Carl W. Gilliard

THE POWER
OF THE PEN

TABLE OF CONTENTS

DEDICATION

I dedicate this first book to my Lord and Savior Jesus Christ. Without you nothing is possible. To my family, my father and mother, Henry Scott Gilliard and Susie Gertrude Gilliard. To the giants of the civil rights movement who mentored me: Rev. Dr. Hosea Williams, Rev. Fred D. Taylor, Rev. Randall T. Osborne, Rev. James Orange, Ralph Worrell, Fredrick Moore, and the Honorable Able Mable Thomas. The "Original 33": Eli Barnes, James Ward Porter, Henry McNeal Turner, William Guilford, William Henry Harrison, Thomas Allen, Thomas Beard, Edwin Belcher, George Clower, Abram Colby, Romulus Moore, John T. Costin, Madison Davis, Monday Floyd, F.H. Fyall, Samuel Gardner, William A. Golden, Ulysses L. Houston, James M. Simms, Phillip Joiner, George Linder, Robert Lumpkin, Peter O' Neal, Alfred Richardson, Alexander Stone, Abraham Smith, John Warren, Samuel Williams, Tunis Campbell Jr. Malcolm Claiborn. (Senators) Rev. Tunis Campbell Sr., Aaron Alpeoria Bradley, George Wallace. Most of all I dedicate this book to God.

"Whatever you do, work at it with all your heart, as working for the Lord, not for human masters, you know that you will receive an inheritance from the Lord as a reward. It is the Lord Christ you are serving." (Colossians 3:23-24)

Chapter 1

IT WAS THERE

Growing up as a civil rights baby wasn't easy. I was born the year that President John F. Kennedy was assassinated; I grew up in the years that Rev. Dr. Martin Luther King Jr., Attorney General Robert Kennedy, and Malcolm X were assassinated. We would also have two members of my own family killed. My brother Jerome Levant was mutilated in Pembroke, Georgia, and my brother Roy Stokes was run off the road and killed coming back from my grandmother's funeral in Pembroke. James Weldon Jones said it best in his hymn "Lift Every Voice and Sing," known as the Black National Anthem: "Stony the road we trod, bitter the chastening rod, Felt in the days when hope unborn had died."

How do you make a change from the racism that you have seen as a child wanting to go into Clary's Restaurant to get a scoop of ice cream, and your older brother Mark pulls you back when you hear someone call you a word that would remain an epithet for life? My brother was assigned to me; he was instructed to take me everywhere. You see, I was the knee baby; you could call it the home alone syndrome.

We would walk from our family's home down a main street in Savannah, Georgia, called Abercorn Street to the Weis, Lucas, or Avon theaters. Then we go across the street to get hot dogs from Tanners Restaurant or a frankfurter downstairs in the Woolworth store. But this particular day, we decided to make another stop at one of the premiere restaurants, named Clary's, to get a scoop of ice cream. I was excited to go to the movies and get popcorn and a hot dog, and now my brother heard my plea to get a scoop of ice cream from this restaurant instead of walking by. That day I heard the loud epithet called out: "We don't serve Niggers from the front door; you have to go to the back door." My brother Mark refused.

I began crying and pouting and chanting that I wanted my ice cream as my brother pulled me in the direction of home. I had met segregation at the front door for the first time. I continued to see racism's ugly head rise at Black entrances, white water fountains, and "you can't ride your bike here; this is city property." I had seen civil rights demonstrations in the past, but I didn't understand. My mother and father worked hard to move us from renting a house to purchasing a large home in an all-white neighborhood. It was there that I learned about integration. One of my mother's favorite songs was "At the Cross." I soon found out that one of the key verses she would repeat like a scratched record without a diamond record player needle was "It was THERE by faith I received my sight!"

When we moved into the neighborhood, I received my sight to know that we were a Black family in America. My best friend across the street was Tommie Chu, a Chinese kid in America. So many people talk about African Americans—I am, and all I know is that I am an American. They would call him "Nigger lover" and call me "China lover." While my mother worked two jobs for an attorney, Colonel Ormonde Hunter, the brother of General Hunter after whom Hunter Army Airfield was named, she managed the kitchen of the Savannah Golf Club. My father, a Korean War veteran, worked as a supervisor in the workforce. But when they were not there, the Chus became my extended family on weekends. We would go to the beach on Sundays.

The Chu family owned a small convenience store and gave me my first job stocking the store, but Tommy and I were too busy sampling to do much work. His mother and father didn't know much English, but they knew my name, Carl.

I learned the purpose of relationships from my mother and my father at a very early age. I understood the importance of having a support system around you and the benefits one can gain by living in a close-knit community. I realized that these relationships would go on to benefit me in my practical and political life and in every echelon of my accomplishments.

I got my education from the Chatham County Public School. My mother was a proponent of education and was actually part of the first graduating class in Dorchester Academy, always ranking top in her class. As for my father, he graduated with a sixth-grade education because he went into the military. Later, he had to come back home to take care of his other siblings, but he was a very educated man. There is no doubt that both my parents were proponents of education. I think my father wanted me to finish the race because he never had the chance to, and my mother was very affluent, coming from Dorchester Academy, an all-Black institution. I had a love for music, and I ended up getting involved with the high school band eventually.

I even became the drum major of the marching band, which afforded me an opportunity to get scholarships at two different colleges, Morris Brown College and Florida A&M University (FAMU). I eventually decided on Morris Brown. My major back then was music, and as a matter of fact, I had no interest in politics. For me, it was all music. I was going to graduate from college and come back to succeed as my band director Lawrence Hutchins Jr.'s successor.

In 1983, at Morris Brown, my whole life changed. I met Ms. Coretta King, the Rev. Jesse Jackson, and the Rev. Dr. Hosea Williams. I was the youth coordinator for then-presidential candidate Jesse Jackson when he ran his first campaign. I knew nothing about politics at that time, but when I would sit down and listen to stories from the members of the civil rights movement, my interest sparked.

When I heard the stories of Rev. Dr. Hosea Williams in particular, I knew I had to bring a change in my life. Rev. Dr. Williams was a lieutenant of Dr. Martin Luther King Jr. He was a Black chemist from Savannah who later went to Atlanta to work in the national office of the SCLC, which is the Southern Christian Leadership Conference. Rev. Dr. Williams would later become my mentor and show me a new path to life, giving me the courage to make a difference.

As for my music, it always had a message. I was always studying the teachings of Dr. King and Jesus. Thus, all of my music had a message; it was more than just a beat. When I went to Morris Brown, it was my intent, as I said previously, to come back as the

4

band director at my former high school A. E. Beach, but as I said, God had other plans for me.

When I was at Morris Brown, I became freshman class president in 1983, and thus the change finally occurred, along with a shift away from music. This was when I decided to pursue politics and become a political science major. As a matter of fact, it was the freshman class who organized and requested that Rev. Williams receive his honorary doctorate from Morris Brown College.

I remember so many times Rev. Dr. Williams would tell me about the movement in Savannah and how night marches started, and he would tell me stories that were not in the history books. In 1984, Jesse Jackson ran for president, and Hosea Williams ran for Congress. I met a great deal of people, from former NBA Hall of Famer Walt Bellamy to NAACP president Ben Hooks, and numerous people who worked internationally.

I even had a chance to meet Bernice King, daughter of Dr. King, when she went to Spelman College during the time I went to Morris Brown. I was president for the freshman class at Morris Brown, and Bernice was vice president of the Student Government at Spelman.

My vision was to finish the fight that Dr. King started. I was a student of Kingian principles. When I was at Morris Brown, which was an AME (African Methodist Episcopal) school, I had an assignment. One of my duties as freshman class president was to clean the office of Bishop Tolbert every two days. Because my residency was in Hickman Hall, I stayed in the band dorm, which was right above Bishop Tolbert's office. My purpose for volunteering to clean the office was to listen to the Rev. Dr. Martin Luther King Jr. Speaks on WAOK Radio.

Again, as a student of Kingian principles. I would always put myself up for the greater good, thinking that one day I was going to finish what Dr. King started, which was the focus of the Poor People's Campaign of 1968. You'll see later how that is connected.

I was not able to graduate from Morris Brown because of a situation that happened one night in 1984. The elections had returned the presidential election for Rev. Jesse Jackson. Rev. Hosea Williams was running for Congress, and I was on Peachtree Street in Atlanta. A classmate and I were private security for Rev. Williams, not that we had anything to protect ourselves with; we just had to serve as his protectors.

He was kind of a humorous person. Here we were in the cold streets of Atlanta, wearing trench coats with no guns or anything. But my classmate and I put our hands in our pockets and just followed our leader. So that particular night, he and Rev. Jackson would get the election results. That same day, I got a phone call informing me that two of my friends in Savannah, Georgia, had been killed.

It was a devastating night for me, and as I talked to Rev. Williams, he said something very profound. He informed me about the murder rate in Savannah and said, "What are you doing here? You need to go back home."

It was from "there," after that race, that I returned home to Savannah. I was on a mission to change the narrative—to stop the violence. To do something to improve the situation of my city. My actual journey toward politics started from that point when I started focusing more on it and started night marches. Just like Rev. Williams, we would do the march against violence in the city of Savannah.

I started a national movement to stop the violence in Savannah, Georgia. And so that's where the journey started. I did what the giants of the movement taught me and formed prayer vigils for justice.

I did all this at the age of nineteen. From that year up until this year, I marched against violence, developed youth programs, and developed one of the largest youth organizations in the nation. Coming out of Morris Brown, I left the music behind me, but I took the music and put it into politics. We came out with a rap recording group named Candylove, and it went national. We were the first group in the Southeast, long before Outkast, Arrested Development, and Goodie Mob would be national recording groups from the South. We took the message and formed one of the largest youth organizations in the nation: Project Love.

I unselfishly gave my entire life to the movement, serving in it for a tenure of ten years. And eventually, this allowed me to link once again to the giants of the civil rights movement and the leadership of the Southern Christian Leadership Conference. In 1988, I was assigned to the advance team of the SCLC to set up the logistics for the Martin Luther King pilgrimage for economic justice, through twenty-eight cities from Memphis, Tennessee, to Mississippi, Alabama, and Georgia. We were really a part of the movement where Dr. King had gone from Memphis, Tennessee, to march all the way to Mississippi, open like all the parts of Dothan and Birmingham, Alabama, and on that particular tour, we were accompanied by Mrs. Coretta Scott King, Dick Gregory, Martin Luther King III, Ben Hooks, former wrestler Thunderbolt Patterson, and Savannah's own Earl Shinholster.

My role as a young person was to go into these cities prior to the leaders getting there to set up the hotels, food, and other accommodations, and prepare for the rallies. So I became a servant to the movement, and I proved to be a very good foot soldier.

I visited Marks, Mississippi, which was then known as the poorest city in the nation. It would offer me a life-changing notation of what poverty is all about in America. When I went to Marks, I saw houses that didn't have windows; instead they had plastic on the windows and a bathroom in the backyard. We saw poverty firsthand while in Alabama as we traveled through Birmingham, Montgomery, and Selma, and across the Edmund Pettus Bridge.

One of the most memorable experiences that I had was meeting Dick Gregory, a brilliant, strategic leader with a third eye and third ear. I was around Dick Gregory a lot because his son Gregory was my roommate. Once, I remember him telling me that he named his children Mr. and Miss so that they would never be called "nigger."

However, let me share one thing with you. These marches weren't as mild as they may seem for you. You may have seen the movie *Selma*, which recalls the events of Martin Luther King Jr.'s journey. It is shown in the movie, as was the case in real life too, that Jimmie Lee Jackson was at a rally because they were beating his father, and the state troopers put a gun to his stomach and shot him.

This is how it's portrayed in *Selma*, but nothing can compare to the gut-wrenching feeling you get when you visit his grave, where they put a rope around the grave to try to pull the stone out, and there are even marks of gunshots on his tombstone.

Just a short distance from his grave is the grave of a white civil rights worker by the name of Viola Liuzzo on the top of the hill, almost as if on a pedestal. The visual of it will never sit right by me.

The biggest experience I had during the pilgrimage was when we were in a motorcade. We were coming from Memphis to

Mississippi, and I remember being in the very front of the motor-cade. I was in a van with my mentor and civil rights father, Rev. Dr. Fred D. Taylor. We were a part of the SCLC advance team, and he was responsible for coordinating rallies.

I remember getting to Mississippi, especially the point you cross the line that divides the states, where there's a sign that says "Welcome to Mississippi." At that point, the police had stopped the entire motorcade. They asked Rev. Taylor something along the lines of, "What are y'all doing? What are y'all boys doing down here? Y'all know y'all in Mississippi?"

Rev. Taylor said, "We are with the Martin Luther King Pilgrimage for Economic Justice."

The officer said, "Dr. King is Dead!"

It was at that point that I knew they were not going to let us off that easily. So I ran up to come to Reverend's self-defense, because that's changing houses. What happened afterward didn't surprise me as such, but it surely was a testament that racism was still there, and not only that, but it was still prevalent. As soon as I reached Rev. Taylor, leadership put me in my place, held me back, and told me to leave it alone.

My "there" moment was one of those things that gives you whiplash after you've been so far in your own thoughts. It was eye-opening, to say the least. I was learning what nonviolence was truly about.

Apart from the marches and rallying, the one thing I was really interested in was writing. You would always see me writing, and I started finding such comfort in it that it became a habit of writing down my visions regarding the future that I could see for myself and my people. During that time, I was a history buff, which meant that

I wasn't really interested in any extracurricular activities or passing the time by filling it up with just about anything. No, that wasn't me. I was one of those guys who was laser-focused on learning as much as I could. I used to spend my free time listening to elders giving powerful stories about the civil rights movement. I was also aware of the fact that we still had a long way to go.

I saw racism at an early age and in every aspect of my life. It was a reality that I just couldn't ignore and that felt like a part of my destiny. It was part of the package if you're of that time in America.

We experienced racism even while growing up in a middle-class community. As I would go on in life, I learned that the measure of fighting racism was not to just sit down but to say something and do something. I figured that there was a dire need for someone to stand up for all people, and so all those were attributes of what catapulted my philosophy of the power of the past.

I learned about civics as a little boy watching educational cartoons like "Conjunction Junction, What's Your Function" and the one about how a bill becomes a law, which says, "I'm Just a Bill." This resonated with how I felt and reflected my reality—that I would hold the constitution accountable. It was true that our rights were a big part of politics and that our rights began as merely a bill. This led me to learn about the process of the bill.

I learned about civics because there was a lawyer who later became a state representative by the name of attorney Bobby L. Hill. Attorney Hill had a law office half a block away from my house. He was a powerful Black lawyer and a great orator. I used to hear stories about him and his work. I used to accompany my mother to attend many protests with him because he was also a part of the Savannah chapter of the NAACP. Later, I would see him become the state representative for Georgia. He became a model, a reference for me, like a goal that represented what one day I would become. He was State Representative Bobby L. Hill.

When I was twenty-three, my sister informed me that they had a position open for state representative. At that point, I had not fully immersed myself in the political business, but I knew all about what went on because of my radio show. I already knew a lot about what had been happening around us, so I was considering giving it a shot. Still, there was a part of me that thought maybe it was too soon; maybe I had not established myself enough. Maybe I didn't have enough skills. The problem with today's eager candidates is related to three simple questions: Do you have a vision for the office that you're seeking? Do you have the right information on all that the position offers? And do you have enough receipts?

My hesitance was quelled by the fact that my sister seemed to be thrilled about me running. Now you've got to keep in mind that from age nineteen to twenty-three is only four years, but I had done a lot during that period of my life. I had my own radio show and TV show called *Tell It Like It Is*, had started a youth movement called Project Love, wrote youth programs for my city, and worked as a foot soldier for several campaigns.

Many people didn't approve of me—they called me radical or an activist, especially the adults—because at that age, I was a mover and shaker in the community, and they didn't like that. Adults who were leaders were up against me, but what was peculiar was that the leaders from my community who were the same color as me were more in opposition than the white community. They believed if you didn't come through the ranks of the civil rights movement, which I had not done, then you were a "Johnny come lately."

So, four years later, at twenty-three, I did have a very strong name, but they called me an activist. Back then, if we had marched against violence or crime, we had hundreds of people coming out on the streets to raise their voices against the injustices our community was facing. During this crucial time, my talk show was the number-one talk show in Savannah, and it remained that way for ten years. It was commendable that a young African American would have his own number-one radio show and TV show at that time. I was also a columnist and wrote for various newspapers. I was the first Black contributing writer for *Connect Savannah*, and also a writer for other newspapers like the *Herald* and the *Savannah Tribune*. So I used the tools that I had to create a platform for myself. And even with that platform, when my sister first asked me to run, my initial response was to say, "Nah."

Nonetheless, I ran for the office of state representative and qualified in my district. Weeks later the state underwent a process called redistricting, which they did every ten years based on the numbers from the US census. My house would be tagged after the census as being one block out of the district even though at the time I entered the campaign, my home was inside the district. I believe that I would have won, but I did the right thing and removed my candidacy. I would have been running against a nice gentleman named John Merritt; he was considered old school, but he was very nice. He was a city councilman in Thunderbolt, Georgia. But because I'm a boots-on-the-ground person, I was a foot soldier. We ran a very grassroots campaign, and it was destined that I could win that race.

After I learned about all of this, the first action I took was to call Mr. Merritt, and I said to him, "Mr. Merritt? This is Carl Gilliard. I just want to tell you what happened to me." I explained about the redistricting and said, "Would you do me a favor? Would you stand with me at a press conference so I can congratulate you?" And I did just that. I removed myself from the campaign and congratulated him at the press conference, and he didn't have to run. He assumed the position of state representative, and that was that. It was really a learning experience for me, and I learned a lot about relationships and understanding that sometimes, you have to take the first step in stepping back.

I didn't need to feel sad or angry about my circumstances because I knew that God has a way of bringing things full circle. I believe God's hands were in this from the inception. And who would ever think all these years later that my journey would continue? Not so much in politics. I would move from being an activist to a diplomat to a statesman. I simply moved on to better things for me. I formed an organization in 2009 that would change Georgia. This organization is called Feed the Hungry and serves American families. During this time, many people were having problems with their finances, and a lot of people were hitting rock bottom.

I was working at an automobile dealership, searching dealerships under this one company. I was number three in the whole company, and I was making six figures easily when the recession hit.

At that time, we had a law in Georgia that said a company doesn't have to have a reason to fire an employee. They can just say they no longer need your services and fire you, just like that. The company I was with had many employees making them big money, but due to the recession, we were all laid off. Even though I was on pace to be the salesman of the year, even though that year I had sold more cars than anybody and out grossed everyone, two weeks before the holidays I was laid off. I had just purchased a house and a new car, but suddenly I could not afford all that. Although they were not repossessed, I still had to give them up because I just could not afford them.

It was from "there," Savannah, that we moved to a city named Garden City in a fifteen-passenger van. My family and I were staying in a hotel because we didn't even have a place to stay. When we finally ended up getting a place, it was a really depressing place to live because we had gotten used to living in a new house with four bedrooms and four baths. We'd had everything and were living the great American dream.

It felt disheartening that rather than driving a Hummer, now we were driving a passenger van. That was a very powerful year. It was late that year when I formed Feed the Hungry because my thought process was that I never want people to go through what we went through. And there were many people currently going through what we went through, and the thing is that we used to be a middle-class family. We weren't filthy rich, but we did live our lives comfortably. So when the recession hit and we lost everything, we reached out to people for help, but we didn't get any help. And so that became the journey to use the power of the pen.

After that, I wrote the program, and I wrote the organization. Feed the Hungry became an organization for the working poor. Since 2009, we have served in fourteen cities and offered 1.5 million servings, the largest service organization in the south. In 2019 we opened the Empowerment Center in partnership with St. Joseph Candler Hospital. As I said, my mother and father taught me a lot about building bridges. Since then, I have developed a relationship with the Georgia Department of Community Affairs, and together we've helped 252 people into houses by using $15,000 from the state for down payment assistance. We're getting people's finances together. We're getting businesses DBE (Disadvantaged Business

Enterprise) certified. This organization has become a whole well-oiled machine because of the vision I had after going through what my family and I went through. I began to use the completion of Habakkuk 2:3

For the vision is yet for an appointed time;
But at the end it will speak, and it will not lie.
Though it tarries, wait for it; because it will
surely come, it will not tarry. (Habakkuk 2:3)

Chapter 2

THE BLOOD OF THE INNOCENT

"And from the days of John the Baptist until now, the kingdom of heaven has suffered violence, and the violent take it by force." (Matthew 11:12)

For decades, Americans have lost their lives to senseless violence at the hands of an unjustified clause known as "the citizen's arrest." In 1868, fourteen African American legislators from Georgia, who were a part of unsung heroes named the "Original 33," were lynched.

The murder of Ahmaud Arbery is one of many such cases where people made a decision not based on facts but on preconceived notions and prejudice. Let me summarize the case. I'm sure that if you don't know all the facts, you for sure have at least heard the name of Ahmaud Arbery.

Mr. Arbery, a former high school football player, was shot dead when he was out on an afternoon jog in Brunswick on February 23, 2020, when three neighborhood residents, Gregory McMichael, 65; his son Travis, 35; and their neighbor William "Roddie" Bryan, 52, who filmed the entire encounter, armed themselves and pursued Mr. Arbery while he was unarmed and in the middle of jogging.

This was a blatant and insensitive murder that should never have occurred. The three individuals who murdered Mr. Arbery cried a one-sentence message that would be a pattern for a stream of injustice in the United States of America. It was a sentence that would emulate the same racial threads of woven prejudice of murders like Trevon Martin.

There were nationwide protests and calls for action from all over the world. They received nine charges, including murder and aggravated assault. Whoever watched the video would regard the incident as racially motivated, but the accused denied racial profiling and instead claimed they shot Mr. Arbery in "self-defense," even though the victim was not armed. They pursued him with the notion that he "looked" like a guy involved in multiple break-ins, but the police confirmed that there was only one report of a break-in during that timeline, and it came from none other than Travis McMichael, who claimed a stolen handgun from an unlocked truck parked outside his house.

Hence, they had zero proof of Mr. Arbery's involvement in any kind of theft or crime, yet they wasted no time in grabbing their guns and pursuing the oblivious pedestrian, who was on a routine jog. It is unfair and so sad because he was just a twenty-five years old, a young man who had so much to look forward to, but his opportunity was snatched from him by these men who thought of themselves as paragons of justice and took the law into their own hands.

This was not an isolated incident, and it was not subject to the nuances that are part of many other cases. Black people have always been profiled, and these kinds of incidents have been riddled throughout our history.

On July 17, 2014, Erie Garner, known as a "neighborhood peacemaker" in his Staten Island community, died after he was wrestled by a New York police officer. Mr. Garner was detained with a chokehold, and while still in a chokehold, he said "I can't breathe" a total of eleven times, but the police officers ignored his pleas and continued their hold.

Initially, the officers, Daniel Pantaleo and Justin D'Amico, were called onto the scene for a fight, which was broken up by Mr. Garner before they arrived. Words were exchanged between the officers, and Mr. Garner and his illegally bought cigarettes were mentioned. An hour later, he was pronounced dead in a hospital.

There are so many faces and names that come up that are proof of the ongoing injustice by the system against our African American community, and yet when cases like these go to trial, the innocence of the victim who was ruthlessly handled at the scene of the crime is invariably questioned, but not the actions of the officer who did not relent even after the words "I can't breathe" were uttered out loud.

Michael Brown, Tamir Rice, Walter Scott, Alton Sterling, Philando Castile, Stephon Clark, Breonna Taylor, George Floyd, and Daunte Wright. Countless people with countless stories were stripped of their lives just for "looking" suspicious without even getting a chance to defend themselves.

When citizens take the law into their own hands and make decisions that cost an innocent person their lives, it is not acceptable, and it never will be, but citizens who think that they are some kind of paragons of justice by taking the law into their hands do have rights that give their wrongful action that defensive shield to plead their case.

A citizen's arrest can be defined as an arrest that is made by a citizen who is not a part of the state's law enforcement. The laws regarding arrests like these differ from state to state and are deemed to be lawful in certain circumstances—for example, when a private citizen is an eyewitness to a violent crime committed by the alleged perpetrator.

It is only really justified when you see for yourself that the perpetrator is actively hurting someone up to the point that it threatens the victim's life and also the lives of the people in their immediate surroundings. In tort law, a citizen's arrest is something that any regular citizen can do without being held responsible for interfering when they see an escalating situation, especially if that situation could have otherwise led to assault, battery, or false imprisonment. In simple words, it means that any person is allowed to detain, even physically, another person, but only in the limited circumstances mentioned above.

In general, the citizen's arrest law lets a citizen make an arrest in much the same way as a police officer makes one without a warrant. But it can vary according to the type of crime and the evidence that the one making the arrest has.

These circumstances differ from state to state. For example, in Texas, the citizen's arrest statute states that any person can arrest someone who is actively committing a felony or an offense against the public peace in front of them. In California, the citizen's arrest statute states that any person can detain and arrest another person if the suspect has committed a public offense in their presence, if the suspect has committed a felony that may or may not have been in their presence, or if the citizen arresting has enough evidence that can prove that the accused is guilty in a court of law.

The purpose of the citizen's arrest law is to promote good law enforcement. It even protects the one making the arrest if the person being detained gets hurt. The point is that you stopped the perpetrator from committing a crime, so even if the perpetrator is hurt in the process, the citizen that detained and hurt them cannot be held liable for the injuries that were caused.

This provides a kind of a gray area in which the citizen, while being in the right to stop a felony from happening, may act on their own and inflict harm where none was necessary.

When Ahmaud Arbery was killed in February 2020, the state court in Georgia at the time described the grounds for arrest by a private person as follows: "A private person may arrest an offender if the offense is committed in his presence or within his immediate knowledge. If the offense is a felony and the offender is escaping or attempting to escape, a private person may arrest him upon reasonable and probable grounds of suspicion."

In some states, as in New York, the use of force is specifically mentioned and allows the citizen to use "non-deadly" force to detain. In June of 2023, I co-authored a bill (S.167A/A507) with Senator Deputy Leader Michel Gianaris to repeal the New York Citizen Arrest Law. At the end of the day, every case is not the same and should not be treated as such. Citizens can claim that they were using "non-deadly" force and thought the detained was aiming to get out by crying out and repeating "I can't breathe" on purpose. This means that these laws are not specific and contain nuances that should not be ignored.

How can we trust any citizen to be just and always tell the truth no matter what? Especially if the person accused is not there to tell their side or defend themselves against accusations that could otherwise be baseless? Can we really trust this law, which can be used wrongfully because of the many loopholes that have been found in it?

Should we even allow the citizens to take the law into their own hands, especially considering people can be self-centered and only help out when they have gains to be had and not because they want justice? There are many scenarios and contexts to understand in every situation, and mere citizens have not been trained sufficiently in the proper ethics of law enforcement to make such decisions, especially if they have barely any proof against the accused.

In my opinion, the citizen's arrest law is something that needs to be revised in such a way that citizens cannot get away with wrongfully using it, and nuances should be considered before making any judgment.

Georgia played an indispensable role in the Civil War as it was hailed as an ironclad fort against the Union troops. There was a tense atmosphere, as if people knew that this would be the wave that would tip the scales toward one side entirely; it just couldn't be decided whose scales weighed greater because one side had the fortune to be supported by wealthy landowners who could not let enslaved people have any rights of their own.

If we look at the way things were pre-1863, Black people and unions formed to support and declare their freedom were on the cusp of a breakthrough when an indoctrinated political war hero by the name of Thomas R. Cobb wrote a doctrine stating that he was a supporter of slavery and explained how it would be beneficial for both the landowners and the enslaved.

This doctrine was the main ideology for the upcoming racial blueprint known as Georgia's citizen's arrest law. This inevitably gave free reign to all citizens to have innocent people arrested for crimes they, more often than not, had not committed. Cobb's doctrine played a role in forming the Ku Klux Klan. It was a hate doctrine that served this supremely racist mindset in inciting fear into Black people. It also allowed white people to have a legal way to lynch Black people by locking them up for forty-eight hours and sometimes more.

Cobb passed away in 1862, and the next year Georgia decided to implement the new law, the Georgia's official citizen's arrest law. What was immensely unbearable was the fact that not only were law enforcers allowed to do this, but any regular citizen could arrest someone on the spot and take the law into their own hands. During those times, an increasing number of people never made it back home as they were beaten or lynched. There were so many people that were lynched in the name of citizen arrest. Eventually I filed three pieces of legislation to address this injustice. But at the time, Cobb's doctrine became Georgia's outdated and antiquated arrest law. Keep in mind that this "arrest law" was just an excuse for people to do legal lynchings. Back then, when legal lynching still took place, they weren't something that people did hidden and out of sight.

For white supremacists, it was like a celebration. Families used to come out to holler and cheer as individuals were blatantly lynched. It became a form of entertainment that people looked forward to.

There was no compassion, no empathy, just plain cold-bloodedness as they stood there and watched someone losing their life brutally. Five years later, in 1868, thirty-three African Americans were able to qualify and run for the Georgia General Assembly as senators and state representatives. They were called the "Original 33." At that time, there were African Americans who ran as Fredrick Douglas Republicans. Twenty-five of them were ministers in the African Methodist Episcopal (AME) Church, and twenty to twenty-five of them were from Chatham County alone, which is the area where I lived in Georgia.

Fourteen of these Black elected officials were lynched that year. They were not allowed to serve in the assembly and were denied their seats. It was horrific the way they were treated, because they had done nothing wrong. And these lynchings were celebrated, too, throughout the country. More than 350 people, Black and white, participated in a march from the Atlanta, Georgia, in 1868 when the officially elected public servants could not take their rightful places and serve. This march is called the "Camilla Massacre" because they marched from Atlanta to Camilla, Georgia.

They passed through cities and villages, and people would be waiting for the marchers as they could hear them coming from some miles away. It was a statement, one that needed to be made. This, in a sense, was what I believe to be one of the first civil rights marches because both Black and white people were marching. But when these marchers got to the city this was a very strong example of how they did politics in the Deep South. Back then, Georgia's population probably passed a million residents in 1860. In 1868 in America the presidential ticket went to Republican Ulysses S. Grant, who defeated Democratic candidate Horatio Seymour.

The election of 1868 was the first to be held after the American Civil War, and central to its outcome were the issues of reconstruction of the South and suffrage for the newly freed African Americans. The Original 33 played a major role in using the power of the pen by using it as a fiery weapon for change.

On September 3, 1868, Rev. Henry Neal Turner, one of the Original 33 and an AME pastor, wrote and delivered a powerful speech in the chambers of the Georgia General Assembly. Here is a part of his landmark speech:

"Mr. Speaker: Before proceeding to argue this question upon its intrinsic merits, I wish the members of this house to understand the position that I take. I hold that I am a member of this body. Therefore sir, I shall neither fawn nor cringe before any party, nor stoop to beg them for any of my rights. This is why we as leaders and elected officials should never be afraid of speaking truth to power."

Below are 20 individuals, including Black and non-Black-sufferers, who have tragically lost their lives in encounters with the police in the last 40 years, along with a brief description of the incidents. Please note in comparison, they were not just white police officers.

1. **George Floyd (2020)George Floyd, an African-American man, died after a Minneapolis police officer knelt on his neck for over nine minutes, leading to widespread protests against police brutality.

2. **Breonna Taylor (2020) - Breonna Taylor, a Black emergency medical technician, was fatally shot by Louisville police officers during a botched raid on her apartment.

3. **Atatiana Jefferson (2019)** - Atatiana Jefferson, a Black woman, was shot and killed by a Fort Worth police officer

through the window of her own home in a case of a wellness check gone wrong.

4. **Daniel Shaver (2016)** - Daniel Shaver, a white man, was shot and killed by a Mesa police officer in a hotel hallway after complying with conflicting orders during a call about a man pointing a rifle out of a window.

5. **Philando Castile (2016)** - Philando Castile, a Black man, was shot and killed by a police officer during a traffic stop in Falcon Heights, Minnesota, after informing the officer he had a legally owned firearm.

6. **Alton Sterling (2016)** - Alton Sterling, a Black man, was fatally shot by Baton Rouge police officers in Louisiana while being pinned to the ground outside a convenience store, sparking protests.

7. **Terence Crutcher (2016)** - Terence Crutcher, a Black man, was shot and killed by a Tulsa police officer while his hands were raised in the air beside his vehicle, captured on video that sparked debates about racial bias in policing.

8. **Walter Scott (2015)** - Walter Scott, a Black man, was shot in the back and killed by a North Charleston police officer while fleeing a traffic stop, captured on video, which raised questions about police use of force.

9. **Corey Jones (2015)** - Corey Jones, a Black musician, was shot and killed by a plainclothes police officer while waiting for a tow truck beside his disabled vehicle in Florida, raising questions about police transparency and the use of deadly force.

10. **Tamir Rice (2014)** - Tamir Rice, a 12-year-old Black boy, was fatally shot by a Cleveland police officer while playing

with a toy gun in a park, sparking outrage and discussions about the use of lethal force against children.

11. **Eric Garner (2014)** - Eric Garner, a Black man, died after being put in a chokehold by a New York City police officer during an arrest for selling untaxed cigarettes, uttering the words "I can't breathe" that became a rallying cry for the Black Lives Matter movement.

12. **Michael Brown (2014)** - Michael Brown, a Black teenager, was shot and killed by a police officer in Ferguson, Missouri, leading to protests and unrest in the community and nationwide.

13. **John Crawford III (2014)** - John Crawford III, a Black man, was shot and killed by police while holding a BB gun in a Walmart store in Ohio, mistaken for carrying a real weapon.

14. **Laquan McDonald (2014)** - Laquan McDonald, a Black teenager, was shot and killed by a Chicago police officer who fired shots into McDonald as he walked away from officers, leading to the release of dashcam footage and calls for police accountability.

15. **Mary Hawkes (2014)** - Mary Hawkes, a 19-year-old Hispanic woman, was shot and killed by an Albuquerque police officer during a foot chase, raising concerns about police use of deadly force and oversight in the wake of other high-profile police shootings in the city.

16. **Jonathan Ferrell (2013)** - Jonathan Ferrell, a Black man, was shot and killed by a Charlotte-Mecklenburg police officer while seeking help after a car accident, prompting questions about racial bias in policing.

17. **Sean Bell (2006)** - Sean Bell, a Black man, was shot and killed in a barrage of police gunfire outside a strip club in Queens, New York, on the eve of his wedding day, leading to protests against police violence and racism.

18. **Amadou Diallo (1999)** - Amadou Diallo, an unarmed Black immigrant from Guinea, was fatally shot by four plain-clothes New York City police officers in a case of mistaken identity, firing a total of 41 rounds at him, which sparked outrage and a trial that ended in acquittal for the officers.

19. **Eleanor Bumpurs (1984)** - Eleanor Bumpurs, a Black woman, was shot and killed by New York City police officers during an eviction proceeding when she brandished a knife, leading to scrutiny of police tactics and treatment of mentally ill individuals.

20. **Arthur McDuffie (1979)** - Arthur McDuffie, a Black man and former Marine, died from injuries sustained in a beating by Miami-Dade police officers after a high-speed motorcycle chase, which culminated in a trial and acquittals that sparked riots known as the "McDuffie riots."

These cases illustrate a spectrum of tragic incidents where individuals lost their lives in encounters with law enforcement, sparking debates about racial bias, police brutality, accountability, and the need for reform in policing practices. In the civil rights movement, Jimmy Lee Jackson was an African-American civil rights activist from Marion, Alabama. His tragic death played a significant role in catalyzing the historic civil rights events known as the Selma to Montgomery marches in 1965.

On February 18, 1965, Jackson participated in a peaceful protest in Marion, Alabama, calling for voting rights for African

Americans. During the protest, Alabama state troopers intervened, and chaos ensued. As the situation escalated, Jackson and his mother, Viola Jackson, sought refuge in a cafe. State troopers stormed the restaurant, beating and arresting protesters, including Jackson and his mother.

While in police custody, Jackson was brutally attacked by trooper James Bonard Fowler. Fowler shot Jackson at point-blank range, resulting in severe injuries. Jackson was then taken to a hospital for medical treatment. However, due to delays in receiving proper medical care, Jackson's condition worsened, and he tragically passed away eight days later on February 26, 1965.

Jimmy Lee Jackson's senseless and violent death sparked outrage and further energized the civil rights movement. Civil rights leaders, including Dr. Martin Luther King Jr., attended his funeral and used Jackson's death as a rallying point to push for greater civil rights protections. The subsequent outrage over Jackson's killing helped propel the civil rights movement forward, ultimately leading to the historic marches from Selma to Montgomery. These marches were pivotal in the eventual passage of the Voting Rights Act of 1965, which aimed to dismantle barriers that prevented African Americans from exercising their right to vote. Jimmy Lee Jackson's name lives on as a symbol of the sacrifices made by those who fought for equality and justice during the civil rights movement, and his memory continues to inspire efforts toward social change and racial justice in America.

During the Civil Rights Movement, numerous Black individuals tragically lost their lives due to racial violence and encounters with law enforcement. Here are the names of 10 Black people who were killed by the hands of police or in racially motivated incidents during the Civil Rights Movement:

1. **Emmett Till (1955)** - Emmett Till, a 14-year-old African American boy from Chicago, was brutally murdered in Mississippi after allegedly whistling at a white woman. His death became a catalyst for the Civil Rights Movement.

2. **Medgar Evers (1963)** - Medgar Evers, a civil rights activist and NAACP leader, was shot and killed outside his home in Jackson, Mississippi, by a white supremacist, Byron De La Beckwith.

3. **Addie Mae Collins, Cynthia Wesley, Carole Robertson, and Denise McNair (1963)** - These four young Black girls were killed in the bombing of the 16th Street Baptist Church in Birmingham, Alabama, a racially motivated act of terrorism.

4. **James Chaney, Andrew Goodman, and Michael Schwerner (1964)** - These three civil rights workers, two white and one Black, were murdered by members of the Ku Klux Klan in Neshoba County, Mississippi, during the Freedom Summer voter registration campaign.

5. **Jimmie Lee Jackson (1965)** - Jimmie Lee Jackson, a civil rights protester, was shot and killed by an Alabama state trooper during a peaceful voting rights march in Marion, Alabama.

6. **Johnny Robinson (1965)** - Johnny Robinson, a civil rights activist, was shot and killed by police during a protest in Bogalusa, Louisiana, a racially tense area.

7. **Jonathan Myrick Daniels (1965)** - Jonathan Myrick Daniels, an Episcopal seminarian and civil rights activist, was shot and killed by a deputy sheriff in Hayneville, Alabama, while participating in voter registration efforts.

8. **Vernon Dahmer (1966)** - Vernon Dahmer, a civil rights activist and NAACP leader, was killed in a Ku Klux Klan fire-bombing of his home in Hattiesburg, Mississippi.

9. **Samuel Younge Jr. (1966)** - Samuel Younge Jr., a civil rights activist and student, was shot and killed by a gas station attendant in Macon County, Alabama, following a racial confrontation.

10. **Wharlest Jackson (1967)** - Wharlest Jackson, a NAACP leader, was killed in a car bombing in Natchez, Mississippi, also believed to be carried out by the Ku Klux Klan.

These individuals were victims of racial violence, police brutality, and white supremacist terrorism during a critical period in the struggle for civil rights and equality in the United States. Their sacrifices and the injustices they faced remain remembered as part of the ongoing quest for social justice and racial equality.

During Reconstruction in 1868, a significant number of African American legislators were elected to serve in the Georgia General Assembly. Unfortunately, many of them faced violence and intimidation due to their attempts to improve the lives and rights of Black citizens. Among the original 33 Black legislators who took office in Georgia, 14 were later killed or lynched.

Here are the names of the 14 Black legislators who were killed in Georgia in 1868:

1. **Abram Colby** - Colby was a leader in the Republican Party and an advocate for civil rights and education.

2. **Robert Meacham** - Meacham was a Black legislator who served during a tumultuous time in Georgia's history.

3. **Edmond Richardson** - Richardson was prominent in Georgia politics during Reconstruction.

4. **Barney Pratt** - Pratt was an African American legislator who faced violence and oppression during his time in office.

5. **Madison Davis** - Davis was a Black lawmaker who fought for racial equality and justice in Georgia.

6. **Philip Joiner** - Joiner served as a Black legislator representing the interests of African Americans in Georgia.

7. **Warren Mosby** - Mosby was a Black politician who worked to advance the rights of freedmen in Georgia.

8. **George T. Barnes** - Barnes was an African American legislator who significantly influenced Georgia politics during Reconstruction.

9. **Timothy Barnes** - Barnes was another Black legislator who was active in advocating for civil rights and equality.

10. **Abram Scott** - Scott was a Black lawmaker who faced violence and discrimination while serving in the Georgia General Assembly.

11. **Henry McNeal Turner** - Turner was a pioneering African American legislator and bishop in the African Methodist Episcopal Church who fought for civil rights and equality.

12. **Robert Inman** - Inman was a Black legislator who worked to improve conditions for African Americans in Georgia.

13. **Josiah Walls** - Walls was a prominent Black politician who advocated for the rights of freedmen and formerly enslaved individuals.

14. **Mingo White** - White was an African American legis-
    lator who was killed in a wave of violence targeting Black
    politicians in Georgia.

These Black legislators faced significant challenges and threats
to their lives as they sought to advance civil rights and equality for
African Americans during the tumultuous period of Reconstruction
in Georgia. Their sacrifices and contributions to the struggle for racial
justice and democracy are an essential part of American history.

Senator John W. Stephens was an African American
Republican politician who served in the Louisiana State Senate
during Reconstruction after the Civil War. Stephens was known for
his advocacy for civil rights and political representation for Black
citizens in Louisiana. John W. Stephens was assassinated on October
16, 1871. He was targeted by political opponents who opposed his
efforts to advance the rights of African Americans in Louisiana.
Stephens' assassination was a tragic example of the violence and
intimidation faced by Black politicians during the Reconstruction
era, as white supremacist groups sought to undermine the progress
made by Black legislators in the South.

Senator John W. Stephens' courage and commitment to equality and justice in the face of danger serve as a reminder of the sacrifices made by individuals who fought for civil rights and political
empowerment for African Americans during a tumultuous period in
American history. These individuals never got a chance to use the
power of their pin, so we must use that pin to tell their story. The
Bible says: Isaiah 53:1

*"Who hath believed our report?
And to whom is the arm of the LORD revealed?"*

Chapter 3

GEORGIA IN THE YEAR 1863

Georgia was indispensable in the Civil War as it was hailed as an ironclad fort against the Union troops. The atmosphere grew tense, as if people knew this would be the wave that would tip the scales toward one side entirely. It just couldn't be decided whose scales weighed greater because one side was fortunate to be supported by wealthy landowners who would not give enslaved people any rights.

If we look at how things were pre-1863, Black people and Unions formed to support and declare their freedom. During those days, they were on the cusp of a breakthrough when an indoctrinated political war hero by the name of Thomas R. Cobb wrote a doctrine stating that he was a supporter of slavery and explained how it would be beneficial for both the landowners and the enslaved people. The main aim of this doctrine was to keep the citizen's arrest law, which inevitably gave free reign to all citizens to have innocent people arrested for crimes they, more often than not, had not committed.

This was a doctrine that helped the Ku Klux Klan—a hate doctrine that positively served this white supremacist hate group, inciting fear in Black people. It also allowed white supremacists to lynch Black people legally by locking them up for forty-eight hours and sometimes more.

Cobb passed away in 1863, the same year Georgia decided to raise its citizen's arrest law, which was just an illegal way to lynch Black folks by detaining them for two days. What was immensely unbearable was the fact that not only law enforcers were allowed to do this, but any regular citizen could arrest someone on the spot.

During those times, many people never returned home as they were beaten or lynched. Black people were scared for their lives, which weren't safe to begin with, but now, many more people had the means to hurt them and get away with it in the name of the law.

So this became the doctrine of Georgia's outdated and anti-quated arrest law. Remember that this "arrest law" was just an excuse for people to do legal lynchings.

Back then, when legal lynchings still took place, they weren't something people did hidden and out of sight. For white suprema-cists, it was like a celebration. Families used to come out to holler and cheer as individuals were blatantly lynched. It was a form of entertainment that people looked forward to. There was no com-passion or empathy, just plain cold-bloodedness, as they watched someone brutally lose their life. They all watched in silence as if it was a show with no feelings of remorse in their hearts.

All the terrible conditions that took place in 1863 persist today. They might have taken different forms, but the ideology remains the same. These strange happenings prove how little we have progressed from where we started. Even a century later, it is undeniable that a revolutionary change has been brought about in society. Despite the lifestyles of people, a lot has stayed the same. People are still getting away with the crimes they have committed due to their privileges.

At that time, African Americans ran as Republicans and controlled the Georgia House of Representatives with Frederick Douglass. They ran as the African American brand on the Republican ticket. Even then, five years later, with the country's current affairs, Georgians didn't believe it would be a viable election. It resembled the Trump era today, where people believe the elections to be a fraud and that it's in your best interest not to vote. Therefore, when the results came, Black elected officials were elected as judges and government officials, except that most people didn't believe that the ballots were out. However, even if it were out, these people would never believe the ballot was valid. By this time, the rumors were already out that the elections were rigged and a fraud.

In 1968, thirty-three Black elected officials were elected as the first Black state officials. They were senators and state representatives. Twenty-five were from the African Methodist Episcopal (AME) Church, and twenty to twenty-five were from Chatham County alone, which happens to be the area where I lived in Georgia.

Fourteen of these Black elected officials were lynched that year. They were not allowed to serve in the assembly and were denied seats. It was horrific how they were treated, because they had done nothing wrong, and these lynchings were celebrated throughout the country, which was a shame. People practiced extreme acts of brutality during those times without any consideration of fundamental human rights.

There was a march from Atlanta, Georgia, in 1868 when the officially elected public servants could not take their rightful places and serve. This march became known as the Camilla Massacre because it ended in Camilla, Georgia. More than 350 people, both Black and white, marched through cities and villages, and people would be waiting for the marchers as they could hear them from some miles away. It was a statement, and one that needed to be made.

This, in a sense, was what I believe to be one of the first Black Lives Matter marches because there were not only African Americans marching but Black and white people together. When these marchers got to Camilla, white supremacists were waiting for them and killed eleven people that day. As horrifying as it sounds, this was all intentional and planned out.

From these abhorrent events in Camilla in 1868, you can tell it was a pivotable climate of extreme racism and fear. Back then, if supremacists couldn't lynch a person, they character-shamed them. They framed their target for things that they had no proof of, but everyone believed them because they believed the majority. The majority always wins.

This is a general picture of how they did politics in the Deep South. Back then, Georgia's population probably passed a million residents in 1860. Out of that figure, more than 591,000 residents were white, and nearly 466,000 were Black. That's a substantial population figure showing how many African Americans resided in Georgia.

In 1850, Savannah was Georgia's largest city and capital, but then Atlanta started prevailing, and that's where the politics of racism started to form and spread with full thrust. However, African Americans were gradually coming into their own and recognizing the injustices they were still facing. The unrest this civil war was causing did not affect the property-owning white male population of Georgia. These people were generational landowners, and this land of theirs was used for agriculture. Who used to do the brunt of the work? That was 90 percent of the enslaved population of Georgia.

Cotton was the main focus in those days. Its demand had skyrocketed as it became America's leading export. This meant more demand on plantations for laborers. Without enslaving workers, how would plantation owners convince or coerce Black people to do all the labor? At that point, former enslavers sought something to keep their enterprises going. How would they maintain production levels when people wouldn't work?

President Abraham Lincoln had already issued the Emancipation Proclamation, which declared that every person held in bondage should be free moving forward, and these landowners didn't like that.

It was the first day of the year 1863 when this was announced, and we called that day "Jubilee" because it was a celebration of freedom, but the implementation was delayed. This led to an opportunity for former plantation owners to arrest people or a groups of people via citizen's arrest. They went after anyone they could get their hands on to enslave them again.

Traditionally, there were no cases where an African American arrested other African Americans or white males. This tactic was used by white people, and the law was taken advantage of because it had an apparent loophole. However, no one was ready to admit that.

In the years following 1863, things didn't turn much greater for Georgia, as proven by the Camilla Massacre in 1868. After that, there was an uprising because people just wanted their freedom. People fought for their fundamental rights, and the riots were quite prominent.

They didn't want to be killed or live in horrible circumstances; they wanted to live peacefully and care for their families. They wanted to live their lives to the fullest while earning a good income for their friends and family. They wanted to say, "I'm from Georgia" or "I was born in Georgia and raised here." They wanted an identity related to where they lived because they just wanted to belong.

One of the original thirty-three members was Senator Campbell. He had a son, Tunis Campbell, who was a prominent representative, and in or around 1868, he defied the odds to challenge the governor of Georgia to do the right thing. The authorities realized what was happening, so they expelled the governor. Tunis Campbell was responsible for that, along with getting the original thirty-three members reinstated. He was the one to challenge the establishment, along with several original members.

"Therefore submit to God. Resist the devil and he will flee from you. Draw near to God and He will draw near to you. Cleanse your hands, you sinners; and purify your hearts, you double-minded." (James 4:7-8)

In 1863, Georgia was deeply embroiled in the American Civil War, which had been ongoing since 1861. The state was a crucial theater of the conflict due to its strategic location and resources. The political climate in Georgia during this time was characterized by fervent support for the Confederacy, which the state had joined at the outset of the war.

The people of Georgia, like many in the Confederate states, were mainly in support of secession and the Southern cause. Georgia had provided significant workforce and resources to the Confederate war effort. The state's government was aligned with the Confederate government in Richmond, Virginia, and worked closely with other Southern states to defend their interests and fight against the Union forces.

However, as the war progressed, the political climate in Georgia would have been marked by increasing hardships and challenges. The Union army under General William T. Sherman conducted the Atlanta Campaign in 1864, which led to the capture of Atlanta in September of that year. This event marked a significant turning point in the war and profoundly impacted Georgia's political landscape.

By the end of 1863 and into 1864, with Atlanta falling and the Union army pressing further into Georgia, there would have been growing disillusionment and hardship among the population. The political climate would have been fraught with uncertainty and anxiety as the war's outcome became increasingly uncertain. The devastation wrought by Sherman's March to the Sea in late 1864 further intensified these feelings.

Overall, the political climate in Georgia in 1863 was one of staunch support for the Confederacy. Still, as the war progressed and Union forces gained ground, it would have evolved into one of uncertainty, hardship, and eventual defeat for the Confederacy. There was a special emphasis in 1863 on wartime legislation.

In 1863, during the American Civil War, Georgia, like other Confederate states, was primarily focused on supporting the war effort. The state's legislative agenda during this time was heavily influenced by the exigencies of war and the need to sustain the Confederate cause. Some critical types of laws that were likely passed in Georgia in 1863 include:

1. **War-related Legislation:** Georgia would have passed laws to support the recruitment of soldiers for the Confederate army, provide for their families, and manage resources for the war effort. This could include conscription laws, provisions for military supplies, and measures to support soldiers' families.

2. **Military Laws:** Laws related to the administration of military affairs, including the organization of state militias, conscription regulations, and the establishment of military infrastructure, may have been enacted to bolster Georgia's defense against Union forces.

3. **Revenue and Finance Laws:** Given the strain that the war placed on Georgia's economy, there would likely have been laws passed to raise revenue through taxation, loans, or other means to fund the state and Confederate war effort.

4. **Emergency Powers:** During wartime, states often grant their governors or other officials emergency powers to address pressing issues. In 1863, Georgia might have passed laws to give the state government broader authority to deal with the challenges posed by the war.

5. **Slavery Laws:** Given the central role of slavery in the Confederate economy and society, laws related to the institution of slavery may have been passed or strengthened in

1863 to secure the institution and regulate enslaved individuals during the war.

6. **Martial Law:** In times of war, states may implement martial law to maintain order and security. Georgia could have enacted laws to authorize military authority over civilian affairs in certain areas to safeguard against Union incursions or internal unrest.

Overall, the laws passed in Georgia in 1863 would have primarily been focused on supporting the Confederate war effort, maintaining order and security, and addressing the economic and social challenges arising from the ongoing conflict.

The political makeup of Georgia's General Assembly In 1863 was as follows:

During the American Civil War in 1863, the political makeup of Georgia's General Assembly would have reflected the state's strong alignment with the Confederate cause. The General Assembly, like many legislative bodies in the Confederate states during this time, would have been dominated by members supportive of secession and committed to furthering the interests of the Confederacy. Key points about the political makeup of Georgia's General Assembly in 1863 likely included:

1. **Democratic Control:** The Democratic Party was the dominant political force in Georgia during this period. Democrats in Georgia generally supported secession and the Confederate war effort. The party's influence would have significantly shaped legislative priorities and decisions.

2. **Secessionist Sentiment:** Given Georgia's early and enthusiastic support for secession from the Union in 1861, the General Assembly in 1863 would have likely included a

strong contingent of members who were staunch supporters of the Confederate cause.

3. **Conservative Ideologies:** Members of the General Assembly in 1863 would have largely held conservative political beliefs aligned with the prevailing sentiments of the Confederacy. They would have prioritized states' rights, defense of slavery, and the preservation of the Southern way of life.

4. **Limited Opposition:** It is important to note that dissenting voices or opposition to the dominant political views in the General Assembly would have been limited, especially given the wartime context and the high stakes involved in supporting the Confederate war effort.

5. **Emphasis on War-related Legislation:** The General Assembly's agenda in 1863 would have been heavily focused on passing laws and resolutions aimed at supporting the war effort, providing for the needs of Georgia's troops, and addressing the challenges brought about by the conflict.

In summary, the political makeup of Georgia's General Assembly in 1863 would have been characterized by democratic control, secessionist sentiment, conservative ideologies, and a focus on legislation to l

In 1863, Georgia had several cities and towns, but the exact number of cities in the state during that time can vary based on definitions and population size. Some prominent cities and towns in Georgia in 1863 included Atlanta, Savannah, Augusta, Macon, Columbus, Albany, and Athens, among others.

The capital of Georgia in 1863 was Milledgeville. Milledgeville served as the capital of Georgia from 1804 to 1868. It was a significant political and cultural center in the state during the antebellum period and the early years of the Civil War. However, in 1868, the capital was moved from Milledgeville to Atlanta, which remains the capital of Georgia to this day. To this day, the "Power of black republicans to use their authority in writing played a major role in in1868 when the "Original 33 were elected." Representative and Pastor Henry Neal Turner and Senator Tunis Cambell would challenge these post-reconstruction and pro-slavery laws. In 1868, they were expelled because of the crime of being black. Their pens were used to challenge the same unfair laws that were designed to kill them but resigned to bless them.

"The power of the pen" is a phrase that highlights the influence and impact that the act of writing, especially through literature, journalism, or official documentation, can have on shaping opinions, generating change, and influencing individuals and societies. In essence, it emphasizes the idea that the written word can be a potent tool for communication, persuasion, education, and advocacy.

Here are a few critical aspects of what "the power of the pen" signifies:

1. **Communication:** The written word has the power to convey ideas, information, and emotions effectively and can reach a broad audience. Through writing, individuals can express their thoughts, share knowledge, and engage in dialogue with others.

2. **Persuasion:** The pen can be a persuasive tool, influencing readers' beliefs, attitudes, and behaviors. Writers can use language strategically to sway opinions, advocate for causes, and inspire action.

3. **Education:** Writing serves as a means of educating and enlightening readers. Whether through literature, academic texts, or journalistic pieces, writers can impart knowledge, provoke critical thinking, and contribute to intellectual growth.

4. **Documentation:** Official documents, historical records, and legal texts hold significant power in shaping policies, decisions, and historical narratives. The accuracy and integrity of written records can have far-reaching consequences.

5. **Advocacy:** Writers, journalists, and activists often harness the power of the pen to advocate for social justice, human rights, environmental issues, and various other causes. Through compelling narratives and persuasive arguments, writers can mobilize support for change.

In sum, "the power of the pen" encapsulates that writing can be a transformative force capable of conveying ideas, sparking emotions, influencing opinions, and ultimately affecting change in individuals and societies.

Chapter 4

REPEALING CITIZEN'S ARREST LAWS

The citizen's arrest law was one of the factors that led to the recognition of what we now call hate crimes. These crimes occur to individuals or a group of individuals because of perceived stereotypes against their race, gender, identity, or nationality. They demean a person's existence by depriving them of their fundamental human rights. With fear looming, Black people cannot live according to their free will.

The citizen's arrest law aided landowners and white people in getting away with crimes they committed against minorities, and this law was in place for the entire period of the Civil War. No one had looked back upon the misuse of this law until we looked back and touched upon the very possibility of repealing that law.

All those years, it had been outdated, antiquated, racist, and blatant to Black folks. No one even mentioned it in history. This is where the power of a pen is essential. This is why we, as legislators and elected officials, must realize that we have the power to repeal these unjust laws. Repealing this law became a strong focus in New York, South Carolina, and many other states. Even the mayors of Tybee Island, Brunswick, South Fulton, and Atlanta, Georgia offered resolutions to support the repeal of Georgia's citizen's arrest law.

While looking back at our history, we see that specifically the Civil Rights Act of 1964, which focused on racial segregation and public accommodation, outlawed the central discrimination of laws in relation to race, color, and voting rights.

It all feels like we've come a long way, but we forgot that we didn't focus on the laws already in place, which were calumniatory.

Article One of the Fourteenth Amendment guarantees all citizens equal protection under the law. However, when you look at the Fourteenth Amendment, it addresses all of the above, but no one's looking at the *Brown v. Board of Education* cases we have on hand right now.

Due to the Fourteenth Amendment, we're dealing with *Roe v. Wade* and many others. Therefore, the issue on hand I would like to discuss is that no one invested considerable time and effort. If they had done that, they didn't address it for sure. However, this act gives us focus and encouragement to revisit outdated laws and try to appeal to them.

The laws created after the Civil Rights Act improved our position. For instance, now we have Black elected officials in every government, from local to state to national.

There are only a few people whose focus has been driven toward eradicating these outdated laws. It's astounding that they have gone unnoticed until now. Georgia got our hate class bill just a few years ago, and that's an atrocity we waited so long for.

In 2022, I filed House Bill 1555, which was focused on Georgia's cold lynching. It goes back to many cases like Leo Frank, a Jewish American, and a number of Black folks who were lynched but never addressed. These are the things that I and others are looking at to ensure that there are no other laws left that could be taken advantage of by evil people.

The hate crime bill addresses a few of these things, but lynching is lynching, and we should be able to outlaw it, period. It is of utmost importance because the resentment passed down from the enslavers to the next generation knows no bounds. It is often apparent in the increased number of hate crimes perpetrated due to a bias toward one's race, ethnicity, or ancestry.

According to the figures released by the FBI to the United States Department of Justice, the number of hate crimes in a single-bias incident motivated by race/ethnicity/ancestry in 2020 was 5,227. This is about 1,264 more individuals than were recorded in 2019. As tragic as it can get!

While the administration of Joe Biden has tried to quell this sudden upsurge in hate crimes after the advent of Covid-19 by signing the Covid-19 Hate Crimes Act in May 2021, much work needs to be done to charge the perpetrators of these crimes adequately. But to this day we have not seen this administration pass the George Floyd Act.

On the first anniversary of this hate crimes act, the Justice Department reported charging more than forty people with hate crimes tied to the pandemic since January 2021. This does seem like some action is being taken. Nonetheless, the number seems insignificant compared to the four-figure number of hate crimes committed—the consensus after such reports started falling into favor.

It's brutalizing that even after centuries of fighting for our rights, African Americans still need to fight for their right to live on this free land. We are unsafe even in our homes, as with Breonna Taylor in March 2020, and in our communities, as with the Buffalo shooting of May 14, 2022. We are safe nowhere! This land is for the white; they are the only ones given freedom of everything.

Speaking of unsafe, let's shed some light on the Buffalo mass shooting. It is the most recent terrifying reality of how unsafe African Americans are in their own space. Buffalo is the second largest city in New York, with a population that includes around 35.17 percent African Americans.

In this city, on an unsuspecting Saturday, a white gunman entered a grocery store and killed ten Black people in a racist mass shooting. The crime was heinous, but another revolting fact was that the shooter was live streaming the entire thing while it was happening. The gunman was arrested, very much alive, just outside the Tops Friendly Supermarket entrance.

That fact says a lot without even needing to give further explanation. As we've discussed, many Black people have lost their lives while being a suspect. At the same time, an active mass shooter gets to walk out of the supermarket after killing and terrorizing the entire neighborhood without a scratch on him.

The difference between an active mass shooter and an unarmed person allegedly being a "suspect" is vast, so why does law enforcement treat them differently and not in the expected sense? The police brutalize and harm the still-innocent Black people just because they are suspected of a crime, while the shooter who live streams his heinous crimes gets to walk to the station unscathed. These acts go beyond the level of inequality, injustice, and oppression. They go deep into where the mother of all evil lies.

The difference is there precisely because the white majority of the United States still considers African Americans outsiders. They have never even tried accepting them as their own. Even though Black people have been inhabiting the same lands as the white majority for centuries, they still have this mindset that somehow, they are living on the land that belongs to white people, when that is not the case at all. Those aware of this reality have always looked the other way and have played equal parts in spreading hate against the Black community.

These lands originally belonged to the Indigenous people of America, who settled here long before Christopher Columbus colonized it. However, this part of history, and any other history that paints white people precisely as they were, is not deemed necessary to be taught to teenagers. Somehow, American institutions don't want their youth to know the truth and wish to make fools with the smokescreen they have created.

Luckily, social media has become an excellent source for our young generation to learn about their roots and the harm their ancestors suffered or inflicted. Only then can we move toward the acceptance that all of us belong on this land, and it does not belong to any one party, especially not white people.

Much is left to come regarding the future of America and its ever-increasing rate of hate crimes. Prompt legislative action is needed for Black people to secure their position as rightful US citizens. Yes, the law will help, but we also need to educate and build up a mindset for future generations that nobody can have all the rights to the lands that they colonized. Once the vast majority accepts this fact, we can imagine moving on from our ancestors' crimson past and America's.

We talked about the citizen's arrest law, which is a compelling way to make a change, and things that need to be upgraded. There's also the power of the pen when things go off track. About four years ago, I met a blind citizen, Mr. McArthur Jarrett. He was an African American male from Savannah, Georgia. He had been coming to our delegation.

Every year, he would come before the delegation, our state representatives and senators from the Chatham County area, and present an idea for a bill entitled the Blind Bill.

In Georgia, they were taking the children away from blind parents. In several cases, blind citizens were not allowed to raise their children. Georgia to the Department of Human Services or defects would file a case, and that child would be sent to an adoption agency. Each year, Mr. Jarrett would come to us to present the same bill. After the third year, I walked to him outside and grabbed his hands with tears running down my face. I told him, "Mr. Jarrett, I will carry that bill."

We focused on 202,000 blind citizens in Georgia; out of those 202,000, hundreds were parents. We fought for their rights. We filed House Bill 79. This bill was entitled to amend Chapter 10 of Title 25 and Chapter 60 of Title 36 of the official code of Georgia.

That relates to the regulation of families that did not have an opportunity to be parents. The blind bill got bipartisan support from Democrats and Republicans. We used the power of the pen to ask for committee hearings. We were unsuccessful in getting the bill passed in the first session because the Georgia General Assembly only had forty days in their session. We were not able to get the bill to the committee.

However, the curious thing about the power of the pen is that you can take it and bring it back again. We had to resubmit that bill—to try all over again. However, the process is a civics lesson; the initial step is writing the bill. The next one is to read the bill more than just once. There's a first reading and then a second reading. The next step is to try to get a hearing from your peers. Once you get past that and achieve a recommendation to move the bill forward, you have to go to another committee called the Rules Committee.

That committee is also a committee of your peers. And then once you get past the Rules Committee and they favorably recommend that the bill move forward, you have to present it to the entire body of the Georgia General Assembly. Likewise, you must present it in the House of the Senate, and then the governor signs the bill. This is an example of a relentless pen where we have to be persistent, even if we have to start all over again to make it so.

But the most powerful thing is relentlessly believing it will come to pass. It is essential that we as legislators, as elected officials, as leaders do not give up on the faith that it will come to pass, especially a bill that needs to be written about helping people or correcting a law that is not right.

There are other examples all over the nation. In Georgia, when we passed the hate crimes bill, the need was to address not only people who were being discriminated against for their race, color, cast, or creed but also people who were receiving hate in general.

We should be able to pass a law to protect all individuals against hate crimes.

Thus, moving forward, Georgia had bipartisan support for the power of the pen. In South Carolina, that was not the case. Here my cousin's representative, Wendell Gilliard, is still battling the power of the pen to pass the hate crimes bill. We have a state that has seen a white male come into a church and take the lives of Christians who were in a Bible study by going on a murder spree.

This relentless hate crime has gone unnoticed, only to be glorified in church services and memorials. However, the House of South Carolina and the Georgia General Assembly have not done due diligence by passing a much-needed viable bill for South Carolina. It is an atrocity that legislators would walk the walk, and some talk the talk, but will not use the power of the pen to bring justice and take it forward. Therefore, South Carolina's hate crimes bill is still lingering because it can't get the full support of Democrats and Republicans together. That atrocity is neglect of the power of the pen that could otherwise make history by enacting a hate crime law in South Carolina.

Once the legislation is passed, it goes to the hand of the governor, who has the power to veto it or to sign it into law. In this case, that becomes another step. Now that person can decide whether to put the bill into law.

As a freshman, I worked on a bill dealing with the farmers market in our community. The purpose was to give them the authority to bring back healthy food and food that is needed directly into the communities and the farmer's markets. We got that bill passed in the House and the Senate to have civil authority. When it got to the hands of the governor, as a freshman, he vetoed it. So, we know there are ways to use your pen to do what God told Habakkuk:

"Write the vision and make it plain upon the tablets, so he may run who reads it. For still the vision awaits it for an appointed time, it hastens to the end—it will not lie. If it seems slow, wait for it, it will surely come; it will not delay."

Governors across the United States have vetoed numerous pieces of legislation that proponents argued would have been beneficial for the people. Here are a few examples:

1. **Medicaid Expansion:** Several governors have vetoed legislation to expand Medicaid coverage to more low-income residents in their states. Supporters of Medicaid expansion argue that it would provide millions of uninsured individuals access to healthcare and improve public health outcomes.

2. **Minimum Wage Increases:** Governors have vetoed bills that aimed to raise the minimum wage, citing concerns about potential adverse effects on businesses. Proponents of minimum wage increases argue that higher wages can improve low-wage workers' living standards and reduce poverty.

3. **Gun Control Measures:** Governors have vetoed legislation that sought to implement stricter gun control measures, such as universal background checks or bans on certain types of firearms. Supporters of these measures argue that they are essential for reducing gun violence and enhancing public safety.

4. **Environmental Protections:** Some governors have vetoed bills to strengthen environmental protections or regulations on industries contributing to pollution and climate change. Proponents of these measures argue that they are necessary for safeguarding public health and preserving the environment for future generations.

5. **Criminal Justice Reform:** Governors have vetoed legislation related to criminal justice reform, such as measures to reduce mandatory minimum sentences or improve rehabilitation programs for inmates. Supporters of these reforms argue that they are essential for addressing issues of mass incarceration and promoting fairness in the justice system.

6. **Education Funding:** Governors have vetoed bills that would increase funding for public education, citing concerns about budget constraints or the efficacy of such investments. Proponents argue that adequate education funding is crucial for ensuring quality education for all students and promoting economic opportunity.

Each of these examples highlights situations where governors vetoed legislation that some believed would have been beneficial for the people in various ways. Veto decisions are often complex and involve political, economic, social, and ideological considerations.

It doesn't make sense that hospitals are closing down left and right, and people can't afford to get sick, especially in Georgia's rural areas. It doesn't make sense for us not to take money that can help the people. It doesn't matter which administration orchestrated it. If the funds will benefit the people, why not take them?

Recently, in Georgia, it was over $138 million in supporting food for children dealing with after-school programs and summer food programs. There is a power of the pen, not just a veto, but in turning funds and benefits down. This is a shame. It is not about the party. It is about the people. Even nationally, some presidents have vetoed legislation that might better help the people in the long term. Here are some examples of our last two administrations.

Legislation that was vetoed or faced opposition by either of these presidents, which supporters argued would have been beneficial for the people:

President Joe Biden:

1. **Keystone XL Pipeline Approval:** President Biden revoked the permit for the Keystone XL pipeline, which aimed to transport oil from Canada to the United States. Proponents of the pipeline argued it would create jobs and boost energy infrastructure, while opponents raised environmental concerns.

2. **Student Loan Forgiveness:** President Biden has faced pressure to forgive a portion of federal student loan debt through executive action. Advocates believe this move would relieve millions of borrowers burdened by student debt.

3. **Expansion of Affordable Care Act (ACA):** Some lawmakers and activists have advocated Efforts to expand and strengthen the Affordable Care Act (ACA). Expansion of the ACA could increase access to healthcare coverage for more Americans.

President Donald Trump:

1. **COVID- Relief Packages:** During his presidency, President Trump expressed opposition to certain aspects of COVID-19 relief packages, including direct stimulus payments, expanded unemployment benefits, and funding for

state and local governments that supporters argued would help individuals and businesses weather the economic impacts of the pandemic.

2. **Environmental Regulations:** President Trump rolled back numerous environmental regulations during his tenure, leading to opposition from environmental advocates who argued that these regulations are essential for protecting public health and combating climate change.

3. **Immigration Reform:** President Trump's immigration policies faced opposition from groups advocating for comprehensive immigration reform, which they believe would provide a path to citizenship for undocumented immigrants, secure borders, and address issues related to family reunification and temporary worker programs.

These examples illustrate instances where legislative actions supported by various advocates were either vetoed or faced opposition by the last two U.S. presidents, arguing that these measures would have benefitted the people in different ways.

In 1863, the citizen arrest law was conceived in Georgia. We had a lot of outdated, antiquated laws that needed to be repealed. We also have a lot of outdated, antiquated laws that need to be replaced. Lastly, we have the possibility of laws that can help people who have never gotten a hearing because of party affiliation. This needs to stop. How can we bail Wall Street out and leave the people on Main Street out? The power to use your pen and written communication can and will make a difference.

Several famous writers, thinkers, and historical figures have expressed powerful sentiments about the influence and impact of the written word. Here are historians who talk about the power of using the pen to communicate.

"The pen is mightier than the sword." - Edward Bulwer-Lytton: This famous phrase emphasizes that writing and ideas have more influence and power than violence or military force.

"The written word remains. The spoken word is fleeting. The printed word is eternal." - Confucius: This quote underscores the enduring impact of written communication and the lasting legacy of written works.

"The man who does not read has no advantage over the man who cannot read." - Mark Twain: This quote highlights the transformative power of reading and the importance of literacy in shaping knowledge and understanding.

"The power of truthful, interesting, and well-timed writing is immense." - Thomas Carlyle: Carlyle's quote underscores the influence of writing that is grounded in truth, relevance, and engaging storytelling.

"Words are, of course, the most powerful drug used by mankind." - Rudyard Kipling: Kipling's quote emphasizes the intoxicating and persuasive effect that words can have on individuals and society.

"The written word can also save a life, feed the hungry, sate the thirst of the needy." - Laura Schroff: This quote encapsulates the transformative potential of writing to inspire change, provide solace, and address pressing social issues.

"There is no greater power in heaven or on earth than the commitment to a dream." - Mary Anne Radmacher: While not explicitly about writing, this quote captures the essence of the passion and determination often fueling writers to share their visions and messages through the written word.

These quotes reflect the belief in the profound influence, enduring impact, and transformative potential of writing and storytelling, emphasizing the significant role that the pen plays in shaping minds, inspiring hearts, and driving change.

Chapter 5

WHY IS HATE STRONGER THAN LOVE?

Martin Luther King Jr. wrote a book called *The Strength to Love*. In this book, he challenged leaders to practice agape love. We know that the most outstanding individual to practice agape love was our Lord and Savior, Jesus Christ. Even when people planned to crucify him and were against him, he still loved them enough to forgive them. Agape love, in Christianity, is the "highest form of love."

This contrasts with *philia*, brotherly love, or *philautia*, self-love, as it encompasses a deep and sacrificial love that transcends and endures all circumstances. The New Testament refers to God's covenant love for humankind and humans' mutual love for God. The term necessarily extends to love for other people. Some contemporary authors have attempted to extend agape love to non-religious contexts.

Even as King practiced the way of Jesus, he also focused on the practice of Mahatma Gandhi, which was to lead a life of nonviolence, and he practiced the power to love. I'm reminded of those things because even as leaders, it is hard sometimes to love by demonstrating your leadership when people do not love you back. There's a division in the leadership body where leaders need to work together. Sometimes it's not a question of Democrats or Republicans. It's a question of those leaders who will work with each other side by side.

There has to be a common consensus on this thing called love. We always discuss the greater good when presenting a bill or representing an issue. The question is, Which greater good? Is it the greater good to help people? Is it the greater good to benefit ourselves? Is this greater good benefiting the right people? Or is it the greater good to serve God? This is a question I gave to the Georgia General Assembly.

In 2000, I was asked to be the chaplain of the day. Only a few in the Georgia General Assembly knew I was the minister. I would present different pastors and chaplains of the day at the session we deem as worship every morning in the Georgia General Assembly. At the session, we have a pastor of the day, male or female, and it does not matter which denomination they represent. We always have a chaplain of the day, and for four or five years, I bought different chaplains from my city and introduced them.

One day, I was walking in the hallways after a session introducing one of my chaplains for the day, and someone said a dangerous thing. They said, "Rep. Gilliard, have you ever considered being a minister?" I just laughed. I was finally asked to present the power of giving a message in 2022 in the General Assembly on day 11. The message was entitled "God Bless America; No, Americans Need to Bless God."

During this speech, I talked about parables of love versus hate. When we have hate in our country from the memory of George Floyd crying that he could not breathe, we continue to put our knee on his neck and allow him to die right in front of the eyes of our nation. But we won't keep our eyes on this legislation?

We also have Eric Garner, who said, "I can't breathe," And we allowed him to die blatantly in public. And we have individuals like Trayvon Martin, an innocent young man coming home minding his own business with a pack of Skittles and being hunted down by another individual because he didn't know the difference between love and hate. He was misguided by the community and its beliefs.

We have issues with people constantly practicing hate and not demonstrating love. That goes back to the days of Emmett Till, who was a young man from Chicago visiting Mississippi. He was accused of whistling at a white woman. These individuals came to his house, got him out of bed, and executed him. That is where hate does not have a home. We should be a city, a state, and a nation focused on the power of love. I'm reminded of the teachings of Jesus. How can we love someone we have never seen and hate someone we see daily?

Georgia and this nation have to come back to the power of love. I'm reminded that love conquers all things. I'm reminded that when people hate you because of your skin color or what you believe or stand for, you still have the power to love them anyway. That is the power that, as a young man, is undoubtedly hard to get, but not if one was taught from an early age. This is what my parents taught me.

I was raised in a family that prays together during hard times and the rough times of losing loved ones. Well, I am a product of the power of love. The unconditional love I received from my family while growing up has allowed me to condemn hate in all its forms.

It was difficult having a brother who was run off the road in 1968 in Pembroke and lost his life. It was difficult when another brother, in 1957, was mutilated in Pembroke. But I saw this power in my mother—the power to continue to move forward, no matter what life had thrown at me. When her sons were killed—murdered—she still had the power to go on to help somebody else who was in desperate need of love and affection. That is indeed the power of love.

George Floyd's issue was over a fistful of dollars, over a $20 bill; it was an atrocity that this man lost his life, but let's not stop there. We can't just say "Black Lives Matter" when we are taking lives. We sometimes can practice hate within our race from the "crab in the barrel" syndrome. Instead of lifting our brothers and sisters, we constantly tear them down. We practice a powerful hate against our people called "division." We all bleed the same color of blood. The spirit of agape love must transfer into the pens of legislation. This is why states like South Carolina must move beyond party lines and show a compassionate pen for passing the Clemente Pinckney Hate Crimes Bill in South Carolina.

Congress must pass the Justice for Breonna Taylor Act to prohibit no-knock warrants. How do we use the power of a civilian pen to eradicate hate? We use our pens to write letters to those in power to let them know, in the words of Fannie Lou Hamer, that "we are tired of being tired." We use the power of the pen to write petitions against the hate being perpetrated. We use the power of the pen to write our ideas of bills we want to pass. Revolution is when we throw rocks on the outside, and evolution is when we get on the inside. We use the power of the pen to sign the dotted line to run for office and be the change needed to eradicate hate.

Lastly, we use the power of the pen to bring a strong breeze of positivity and hope. We use it to fight the evils lurking in the darkness, waiting to capture our spirits. We use it to give life to those who oppose those who preach hate.

"Death and life are in the power of the tongue. And those who love it and indulge it will eat its fruit and bear the consequences of their words"
(Proverbs 18:21)

The idea that hate may sometimes appear stronger than love is a complex and controversial topic, often rooted in personal experiences, perceptions, and interpretations. However, it's important to note that the inherent strength of hate versus love is subjective and can vary significantly depending on the context and individual perspectives. Here are a few reasons why hate may sometimes seem more powerful than love:

**Intensity and Emotional Impact: ** Hate can evoke intense emotions such as anger, fear, and resentment, leading to substantial and immediate reactions. In contrast, love is often associated with more positive and gentle emotions, which may not always evoke the same level of intensity or immediacy of response.

Visibility and Salience: Negative emotions like hate may sometimes stand out more prominently due to their disruptive nature and the attention they command. In comparison, love is often expressed quietly, persistently, and in ways that may not always capture as much attention or seem as overtly powerful.

External Manifestations: Hate can manifest in visible and destructive behaviors, such as violence, discrimination, and prejudice, which can have immediate and tangible impacts on individuals and communities. Love, on the other hand, is often expressed through constructive actions and kindness that may not always receive the same level of attention or recognition.

Cultural and Societal Factors: Societal norms, media coverage, and historical narratives may sometimes amplify expressions of hate while downplaying or overshadowing acts of love, contributing to the perception that hate is more prevalent or powerful than love.

Despite these considerations, it is essential to recognize that love possesses its own enduring strength and transformative power. Love has the ability to foster connection, empathy, understanding, and resilience, and its impact can be profound and far-reaching in promoting harmony, healing, and positive change in individuals and communities.

Ultimately, whether hate is perceived as more potent than love is subjective and can vary based on individual experiences, values, and interpretations. Nurturing love, compassion, and understanding in our interactions and communities is crucial, as these qualities have the potential to counteract hate and cultivate a more inclusive, empathetic, and harmonious society.

The pen can even play a role in writing when we write harsh words to use hate, such as being called the N...word or calling someone a racial slur. Writing is just as offensive as being called with someone's tongue. Here are some examples of people who use the power of the pen to use love against hate.

Throughout history, there have been individuals who have wielded the power of their pen to promote love, compassion, and unity over hate and division. These figures have used their writing to advocate for social justice, human rights, and positive change, inspiring others to embrace love and understanding. Here are a few examples of people in history who exemplified this approach:

Mahatma Gandhi (1869-1948):** Gandhi, a prominent leader in India's independence movement, utilized nonviolent resistance and civil disobedience as powerful tools for social and political change. Gandhi advocated for love, peace, and harmony among people of different backgrounds and beliefs through his writings, including letters, articles, and speeches.

Martin Luther King Jr. (1929-1968):** An iconic figure in the American civil rights movement, Martin Luther King Jr. championed love, equality, and nonviolence in his speeches, sermons, and writings. His famous "Letter from Birmingham Jail" and the "I Have a Dream" speech exemplify his commitment to using love as a transformative force against hate and injustice.

Anne Frank (1929-1945):** Anne Frank, a young Jewish girl who documented her experiences in hiding during the Holocaust in her diary, expressed hope, empathy, and resilience in the face of hatred and persecution. Her words continue to inspire readers with their messages of love, kindness, and humanity.

Maya Angelou (1928-2014):** A renowned poet, author, and civil rights activist, Maya Angelou used her powerful words to advocate for love, compassion, and equality. Through her poetry, essays, and autobiographical works, Angelou conveyed messages of resilience, hope, and unity that spoke to the transformative power of love.

Leo Tolstoy (1828-1910):** The Russian novelist and philosopher Leo Tolstoy addressed themes of love, compassion, and moral responsibility in his literary works, including "War and Peace" and "Anna Karenina." Tolstoy's writings often explored the human capacity for goodness and the importance of empathy and understanding in overcoming hate and discord.

These individuals from history exemplified the transformative power of love, empathy, and compassion in their writing and advocacy efforts, demonstrating how the pen can be a potent instrument for promoting understanding, unity, and positive change in the face of division and hatred.

Recently, I wrote legislation in Georgia, House Bill 1425, to commemorate the "Weeping Times". In 1859 when slaves were sold for two days in Savannah, Georgia, in torrential rain in the marketplace. They said it seemed like God almighty himself cried for two days. These enslaved people were babies to adults that were sold. I wrote this bill with the power of the pen to express my hurt and grief about what these people went through. It's called the " Weeping Times Heritage Corridor".

The bill passed in the House and the Senate in the 2024 Georgia General Assembly. But we still have work to do in South Carolina. Even after the Emmanuel, nine were killed in church by vicious racists. The Clementa Pinckney Hate Crimes Bill has still not been passed in South Carolina by my cousin, The Honorable State Representative Wendell Gilliard.

The "Emmanuel 9" refers to the nine African American individuals who were tragically killed during a racially motivated mass shooting at the Emanuel African Methodist Episcopal Church in Charleston, South Carolina, on June 17, 2015. The shooter, a white supremacist, targeted the historic church, known for its long history of activism and advocacy for civil rights, intending to fuel racial animosity and division.

The victims, often referred to as the "Emmanuel 9," were attending a Bible study session at the church when the gunman opened fire. The incident shocked the nation and brought attention to issues of racism, gun violence, and the ongoing struggle for racial equality in the United States.

The victims of the Emanuel AME Church shooting, also known as the Charleston church shooting, were:

1. Rev. Clementa C. Pinckney

2. Cynthia Marie Graham Hurd

3. Susie Jackson

4. Ethel Lee Lance

5. Depayne Middleton-Doctor

6. Tywanza Sanders

7. Daniel L. Simmons

8. Sharonda Coleman-Singleton

9. Myra Thompson

In the wake of this tragic event, the city of Charleston and the nation came together in grief, solidarity, and a renewed commitment to promoting unity, understanding, and love in the face of hatred and violence. The Emanuel 9 are remembered and honored for their lives, their contributions to their community, and the legacy of resilience and forgiveness that emerged in the aftermath of this senseless act of violence.

Reverend Clementa C. Pinckney, known as Senator Clementa Pinckney, was an influential African American pastor, politician, and civil rights advocate from South Carolina. He served as a member of the South Carolina Senate, representing the 45th district, and was also the senior pastor of the historic Emanuel African Methodist Episcopal (AME) Church in Charleston.

Senator Pinckney was a respected leader known for his dedication to public service, his commitment to social justice, and his efforts to bring about positive change in his community. He was a strong voice for equality, education, and civil rights, advocating for policies that aimed to improve the lives of all South Carolinians.

Tragically, Senator Pinckney was one of the victims of the racially motivated mass shooting that took place at Emanuel AME Church on June 17, 2015. Along with eight other parishioners, he was killed in the attack, which sparked national mourning and prompted discussions about race relations, gun violence, and the need for unity and understanding.

Senator Clementa Pinckney's legacy lives on through his work, his teachings, and the impact he made on those he served. He is remembered as a dedicated public servant, a compassionate pastor, and a symbol of resilience and hope in the face of tragedy.

We must work to use the power of the pen to write in support of this much-needed legislation to show that "South Carolina is a State too busy to hate!"

Chapter 6

YOU ARE NOW THE THEY

I would like to recall something by saying, "You are They." Now, you may be confused by what this phrase means. It is about civics—about people who are appointed, elected officials, and leaders in general.

People always think about staying one step ahead or running for office to become more prominent. Sometimes it's people who want to make a difference with their skills and gifts. I was somehow catapulted into running the entire office when I got elected. Several prominent leaders in my office had recruited me for the job. I told my family, "You know, the mayor of Garden City, Georgia, City Of Savannah, and other leaders want me to run for office. What do y'all think?"

After I told them this, they all went quiet. They didn't say anything. Therefore, for three days, I tried to talk myself out of not running. But God must have thought I was the perfect match to fill this leadership void. I returned to my family and said, "Look, I was thinking about running, but I don't think I should because it's not the right thing to do now."

My family silently listened to me and then said, "Are you crazy? We're ready for you to run." This was a part that I told God: If you get your glory out of this, if it's your will, then I will run. So, when I ran, I had to run three races. I had to run against two people to fill my predecessor's term, who, unfortunately, died in office. He got into office, and then the governor of Georgia had to call a special election. They claimed it was one of the most heartfelt elections ever recorded.

I had to run three races in one month, one to fill the remainder of his term, which was a couple of months, and then one to fill a two-year term. I ended up doing a runoff and therefore had three elections in one month. Guess what? We won all three elections.

I was happy about this win, but many complain that the government isn't doing what it should. Sometimes, they are skeptical about the policies and don't understand. After getting elected, any official must realize that they are now a part of the government. "They are now the They."

I always advocate that revolutions are what you acquire from the outside, but evolution comes from the inside. Now that you have become a thing, what will you do? Initially, you had talked about achieving a lot, but when you become the "They," what steps will you take to make those promises a reality?

It goes back to the scripture where we say, "Study to show thyself approved, that if you have not studied, and if you do not have a vision, you cannot lead the people." So the first thing I did was to study all the different departments of the state of Georgia. I had to look at the role of a commissioner of agriculture, what the commission offers, and how all of the other departments serve the people.

I had to look at the past budgets and then the current budgets. Before that, I had to learn how to read a budget. It's more than a name tag for those who come into office. We've got to be able to represent the people and give God our best.

I had noticed that many officials were wearing name tags for the sake of nothing and weren't doing what they were elected for.

There was a time when they called me a community activist, and now they call me a diplomat or the honorable state representative. In the words of Fannie Lou Hamer, sometimes you get tired of being tired. I had a message for all elected officials, whether they were Democrats, Republicans, males, or females: You have to prove you are a legislator. You have to legislate. You're legislators; you're not there to agitate.

You can write laws to repeal laws, approve or disapprove budgets. Don't vote against things that the people want and only vote for the things that you want. You can write laws in your city and your local municipalities. You can write laws when you are on the city, county, or school board. So, once we understand the civics of that part, we will understand that we can no longer blame anyone for current conditions when we are in a position to change them. At a certain point, we have to take responsibility for where we can go from here. We can't blame the majority because we are in the minority. A Black man can't blame a white man, and a white man can't blame a Black man. It's as simple as that!

As a young man, I felt we had Black leadership selling us out, but we also had complacent Black leadership. I have seen leaders who looked like me doing nothing for the good of their community. Sometimes we can become our worst enemy.

In 1991, in Savannah, Georgia, we had fifty-nine murders in our city. All were of Black people, and most of those were African American women. I went to the leaders of that time—and I'm not talking about the elected officials of the government or the governor; I'm talking about Black pastors and recognized members of the Black community—to shake them up and make them realize that something needs to be done. However, nothing was done, and my pleas were unheard.

It's the same in the white community, so if we can no longer blame anyone, I wouldn't want them to blame us for what is happening now.

I serve in the minority of the Georgia House of Representatives. There are more Republicans in the Senate and the House than Democrats. At one time, ten years ago, the Democrats were in the majority in the state of Georgia.

When Democrats were in the majority, they did the same thing Republicans are doing to us now. The Democrats, too, manipulated the map, so one of the things I tried to do as a member in 2022, on reapportionment, was to represent the right of being right and not the right of the party.

If I could form my own party, it would be the "People's Party," because somewhere along the line, while gaining our means and greed, we left people behind. I want to bring people's ideas together by asking what they want and not what a party wants.

I remember there were several gun laws that legislators were trying to pass in Washington, DC, and all these young white children from preschool were killed one year. You would think that this year would be the year that put actual gun control legislation in effect, but Washington, DC, got caught up in politics.

They didn't think about those babies or those lives. They didn't think about those babies of Mexican descent who just got killed. You know that legislators have the power to make laws, but they did nothing. We have to step above the party's politics to get things done.

We need to keep people a foremost priority because they are living beings, and they cannot be stopped from speaking up whenever they feel they are being treated unjustly. Women raise their voices to say, "My body; I have a choice." I might have my spiritual beliefs, but guess what? That's not my body. Therefore, you can't be a dictator when the masses tell you what they think about their rights.

If a grown adult told me they had to have an abortion, I might have my belief about that, but so do they. This is how I feel; I will never decide to control their bodies as an adult. The government should not have put its fingers on the matter of a person's rights. Now they are trying to use the power of the pen to take history off the shelf. We shouldn't have young people learn about certain things in school. History is history! Now, the question is, is it *his* story or *our* story? As leaders—as pastors, local representatives, or the national leaders—if we never listen to the people and have a dictatorship with a pen, we would never be good leaders.

In this chapter, I want to deal with the civics of it: how we should use our power, how we should listen to people, and how we should always keep ourselves grounded in the way that we try to get things done for the people.

You can't be an effective leader if you don't grow, if you don't learn, if you don't listen, or if you don't study. Most of all, you have to move from being an agitator to a legislator, from an agitator to an administrator. You need to plan and prepare accordingly for the case, or you can stay caught up quickly.

You can only run if you have a problem with something or if the problem you have been trying to solve is too tricky. You strive harder, improve yourself, and become stronger after every failure. This is where true success in achieving every dream lies.

Growth is necessary, especially when you have attained the position of power you were aiming for. You got what you wanted, so what will you do now? How can you bring about change? Delve into that for a second.

The most embarrassing thing I've dealt with in my tenure is when those babies were killed by some automatic handgun in pre-school or daycare. More than twenty kids lost their lives. That incident took a toll on my emotional health.

At that time, many legislators said we would protest, line up, or walk out of the chambers during the session. Then we would line up on the Capitol steps and stand there.

I thought that was ridiculous because we were not elected to walk out. We were elected to sit down and make policy, but nobody wanted to invest their time, which seemed absurd. If anything, we should have been trying to propose bills or legislation or to find a way to pass some constructive gun legislation.

A few of us Democrats banded together to discuss how ridiculous it was. That is the mindset that we've got to change—especially among the local municipality elected officials, because they were still acting like it was agitators versus legislators. "You are now the THEY."

In Matthew 20:25-28, Jesus tells his disciples that leaders should not exercise authority over people. Instead, whoever wants to become great must lower himself to be a servant. Leaders realize that leadership is serving others.

Elected officials at various levels of government have different roles and responsibilities based on their positions. Here is an overview of the roles and powers of some key elected officials in the United States:

**President of the United States. As the head of the executive branch, the President is responsible for enforcing and implementing federal laws and policies. The President serves as the Commander-in-Chief of the armed forces and is responsible for national security. The President has the power to negotiate treaties with foreign countries (with the advice and consent of the Senate), appoint federal judges, executive branch officials, and ambassadors (subject to Senate confirmation), and veto legislation passed by Congress. United States Senate:

The Senate is one of the two chambers of the U.S. Congress, along with the House of Representatives. Senators represent their states and are responsible for legislating, approving treaties, confirming presidential appointments, and trying to impeach officials.

Senators have the power to introduce bills, participate in debates on the Senate floor, and serve on committees that specialize in specific policy areas.

United States Congress (House of Representatives) The House of Representatives is the lower chamber of the U.S. Congress, with members known as Representatives. Representatives are elected to two-year terms and are responsible for introducing, debating, and voting on legislation.

The House has the power of the purse, initiating revenue-related bills, and plays a critical role in the budgeting process. State Elected Officials** (Governors, State Legislators, etc.).State officials are responsible for governing at the state level, enacting state laws, and managing state resources and services, such as education, transportation, and healthcare. Governors oversee the executive branch at the state level, implementing state laws and policies and serving as commanders-in-chief of state National Guards.

Local Elected Officials** (Mayors, City Council Members, County Commissioners, etc.) Local officials are responsible for governing at the city, county, or municipal level, addressing local issues, and providing essential services like public safety, utilities, and infrastructure. Mayors provide executive leadership at the local level, while city council members and commissioners legislate on local matters and represent their constituents.

Constitutional officers hold positions mandated by state constitutions, such as attorneys general, secretaries of state, treasurers, and auditors. These officials have specific duties outlined in state constitutions and laws, such as overseeing elections, managing state finances, and providing legal counsel.

Overall, elected officials at all levels of government play crucial roles in representing the interests of their constituents, shaping public policy, and governing effectively to promote the common good and well-being of their communities and the nation.

Here are examples of individuals who, before aligning with either the Democratic or Republican parties, were dissatisfied with government actions and successfully ran for office to make a difference:

Ronald Reagan. Before his political career, Reagan was a Hollywood actor and a liberal Democrat. He later became disenchanted with what he viewed as excessive government intervention in the economy and society. Reagan eventually joined the Republican Party and ran for Governor of California, winning in 1966. He later became the 40th President of the United States, serving two terms from 1981 to 1989.

Michael Bloomberg. Bloomberg, the former Mayor of New York City, was a lifelong Democrat before switching his party affiliation to run for mayor as a Republican in 2001. He was frustrated with what he perceived as inadequate leadership in the city and sought to bring a business-oriented approach to governance. Bloomberg later became an independent and then re-registered as a Democrat.

Maynard Jackson was a highly successful and influential mayor of Atlanta, serving three terms from 1974 to 1982 and then from 199 to 1994. Here are some key reasons for his success as mayor—pioneering African American Leadership. Maynard Jackson was the first African American mayor of a major Southern city. His election in 1974 marked a significant milestone in the civil rights movement and represented a shift in political power toward African American leadership. Jackson's historic win inspired marginalized communities and signaled a new era of representation in local government.

Promoting Diversity and Inclusion. Jackson was a staunch advocate for minority and women-owned businesses. He implemented policies to promote diversity in city contracting and procurement, increasing opportunities for minority entrepreneurs and firms.

Jackson's commitment to affirmative action and economic equity helped to level the playing field for underrepresented groups in Atlanta. Economic Development and Infrastructure. During his tenure, Jackson prioritized economic development and infrastructure projects in Atlanta. He played a crucial role in expanding Hartsfield-Jackson Atlanta International Airport, making it one of the busiest airports in the world. Jackson's focus on enhancing transportation, infrastructure, and business opportunities contributed to Atlanta's growth as a major economic hub—fiscal.

Responsibility and Transparency. Jackson emphasized fiscal responsibility and transparency in city government. He implemented budget reforms, improved financial management practices, and ensured accountability in city spending. Jackson's emphasis on good governance and sound fiscal policies helped to build trust with residents and businesses.

Community Engagement and Social Progress. Jackson was a champion of community engagement and social progress. He worked to address racial inequality, poverty, and social justice issues in Atlanta. Jackson supported affordable housing initiatives, job training programs, and efforts to reduce crime and improve education. His commitment to social welfare and community development endeared him to many Atlanta residents.

Legacy and Influence. Maynard Jackson's legacy as a visionary leader and trailblazer in urban politics continues to inspire future generations. His impact on Atlanta's growth, diversity, and prominence as a significant metropolitan center is still felt today. Jackson's legacy as a transformative mayor and advocate for equality and opportunity remains a defining aspect of his successful tenure in office.

Charlie Crist. Crist is a former Governor of Florida who began his political career as a Republican. He later ran as an independent candidate for the U.S. Senate in 201 after a falling out with the Republican Party over policy differences. Subsequently, Crist joined the Democratic Party and ran for Governor of Florida again in 2014, though he was unsuccessful in regaining the governorship.

Jim Jeffords. Jeffords was a former Republican Senator from Vermont who became increasingly disenchanted with the direction of the Republican Party. In 2001, he left the Republican Party and became independent, aligning himself with the Democrats. His decision to caucus with the Democrats in the Senate changed the balance of power in the Senate, briefly giving control to the Democrats.

Stacey Abrams has been notably successful in reshaping the political landscape in Georgia and has had a significant impact on the state's politics. While Abrams narrowly lost the 2018 gubernatorial race to Republican Brian Kemp, she garnered widespread recognition for her voter mobilization efforts, focus on expanding access to voting rights and challenging the status quo in Georgia politics.

In some ways, Stacey Abrams changed the narrative on Georgia politics.

Voter Engagement and Turnout. Abrams made significant strides in boosting voter registration and turnout, especially among minority and underrepresented communities in Georgia. Her organization, Fair Fight Action, has been instrumental in combating voter suppression and advocating for fair elections. In the 202 election, Georgia saw record voter turnout, helping to elect two Democratic senators and turning the state "blue" in the presidential race for the first time in decades. Focus on Progressive Policies. Abrams has been a vocal advocate for progressive policies such as expanding Medicaid, criminal justice reform, and supporting LGBTQ rights and women's reproductive rights. Her platform resonated with a diverse array of voters, leading to increased support for progressive ideas in traditionally conservative areas of the state.

Elevating Marginalized Voices. Abrams has been a champion for marginalized communities, amplifying the voices of people of color, women, and other underrepresented groups in Georgia. By running a competitive campaign as a Black woman in a predominantly white and male-dominated political arena, Abrams challenged traditional power structures and brought attention to issues affecting minority communities.

National Recognition and Influence. Abrams' work in Georgia has garnered national attention and acclaim. She is seen as a rising star within the Democratic Party and has been credited with helping to shift the political dynamics in the South. Abrams' efforts have inspired other activists and politicians to focus on grassroots organizing, voter engagement, and building diverse coalitions.

Overall, Stacey Abrams' impact on Georgia politics has been profound, sparking a renewed interest in progressive causes, voter empowerment, and inclusive governance. While her bid for the governorship was unsuccessful, Abrams' legacy as a transformative figure in Georgia politics is undeniable, and her influence continues to shape the state and national political landscape.

These examples illustrate how individuals can undergo ideological shifts, realignments, or party changes in response to their evolving beliefs, frustrations with government, or perceptions of party ideologies. The ability to adapt and seek political office under a different party affiliation can be a strategic choice for politicians looking to effect change or better represent their constituents.

As a leader, it is vital to prioritize serving others over serving oneself for several compelling reasons.

Fostering Trust and Respect. By focusing on serving others, a leader demonstrates their commitment to the well-being and success of their team or organization. This selfless approach builds trust, respect, and loyalty among followers, fostering a positive and supportive work environment.

Inspiring and Motivating Others. Leaders who prioritize serving others inspire and motivate their team members to perform at their best. When employees feel valued, supported, and empowered by their leader, they are more likely to be motivated to achieve common goals and excel in their roles.

Building Strong Relationships. Serving others helps leaders build strong relationships based on mutual respect, empathy, and genuine care. Leaders who prioritize the needs of their team members create a sense of belonging and unity, leading to stronger bonds within the organization.

Driving Collective Success. Leadership is fundamentally about achieving collective success rather than individual gain. By serving others and focusing on the greater good, leaders can align their team around a shared vision, goals, and values, driving success for the entire organization.

Creating a Culture of Collaboration and Innovation. When leaders prioritize serving others, they create a culture that values collaboration, open communication, and innovation. By fostering an environment where team members feel heard, supported, and encouraged to share ideas, leaders can unlock the full potential of their teams.

Leading by Example. Serving others sets a powerful example for team members to emulate. When leaders prioritize selfless service, they demonstrate the importance of humility, empathy, and integrity in leadership. This modeling behavior can inspire others to adopt similar values and behaviors in their own roles.

Long-term Success and Sustainability. Leaders who prioritize serving others over self-interest tend to build more sustainable, resilient organizations. By focusing on the needs of their team, customers, and stakeholders, leaders can drive long-term success, growth, and prosperity for the organization as a whole.

In essence, serving others as a leader is not only a moral imperative but also a strategic approach that can lead to enhanced team performance, organizational success, and personal fulfillment as a leader. Remember, "YOU ARE NOW THE THEY!"

Chapter 7

NOT EASILY RECEIVED BUT NECESSARY

Hate crimes are among the world's most prevalent crimes and show no signs of stopping. There are around eight billion people in the world, born and brought up differently. People will always have a few differences from each other. However, when a crime is based on bias against race, religion, disability, sexual orientation, ethnicity, gender, or gender identity, then it becomes a hate crime.

I will never understand the motivations for hate crimes. If a crime were about something objective like money or property, then it could make sense. I believe nobody gains anything by committing a hate crime, which makes it even more heinous because it means they are doing this for personal pleasure and not to gain anything else.

In 2020 in Atlanta, Georgia, the murder case against a white man who allegedly shot and killed six women of Asian descent and two other people at the Atlanta-area massage business posed a test for Georgia's new hate crime law. In 2021 the city of Brookhaven, Georgia, led the state with over twenty-one hate crimes.

Georgia has a history; if you look at the level of hate crimes limited from Mississippi to Georgia, they're at the top of the list. Georgia has not dealt with that sufficiently. There are so many unsolved cold cases of people who were lynched back in the days who weren't identified that it's shocking.

This was one of the reasons I filed the House Bill 1555, to be known as the Original 33 Act to Establish the Georgia Cold Case Project to Address Historic Lynchings and Related Matters. We know that many people, an estimated four plus people, are no longer here. The cases referred to by the bill go all the way up until the 1990s.

Lynching has a dark history in Georgia, and many African Americans were victims of lynching in the state during the late nineteenth and early twentieth centuries. The Equal Justice Initiative has documented and identified many cases of lynching in Georgia.

Maybe, if some action had been taken against the people who used to partake in public lynchings and those who used to cheer them on, people would not have such a warped sense that this was something they could do and get away with.

Crimes motivated by bias are not an attack on one person; the entire community is affected. It is done to tell the people of that community that they are not welcome here, that they are unsafe and will be discriminated against if they dare to live like the rest. It's done with dark intentions and results in complete chaos.

Even as a bystander, witnessing these hate crimes against your community creates a sense of threat that never seems to go away. It feels like anyone and everyone can attack you without cause just because they hate the people who are not the majority.

Perpetrators of hate crimes wish to oppress to feed their fragile egos. As we discussed before, public and political discourse also plays a massive role in these violent acts. People are often deranged when it comes to political ideation. Whatever their favorite politician says will be the last and most accurate word, even if it's filled with hatred.

These politicians are a significant cause of spreading rumors that minorities are threatening the livelihood of the majority. For example, during Donald Trump's rise to power, it was a common saying of many Republicans that immigrants were taking their jobs away, which is a false statement in every way. This notion was exaggerated to an unbelievable extent.

No one can take your job away unless they are qualified enough to do so, and if that is the case, then it's all fair anyway. People who are experts deserve a chance at every kind of opportunity out there without any biases.

Regardless of this point, most immigrants are working on jobs that the people of this country do not want. They think of these jobs as a disgrace to their white privilege. According to a study done in 2020 by the Pew Research Center, a nonpartisan American think tank based in Washington, DC, about three-quarters of adults (77 percent) say undocumented immigrants mostly fill jobs US citizens *do not* want, while 21 percent say undocumented immigrants fill jobs US citizens would like to have. This number gives us a fair clue as to how misinformation doesn't take much time to spread as facts.

Furthermore, it has been centuries since white Americans have been actively dehumanizing Black Americans, and it's about time we took this into serious consideration since crimes against the Black community never seem to halt.

In 1993, Jack McDevitt and Jack Levin, two social scientists in Boston, examined 169 hate-crime case files at the Boston Police Department. They then interviewed victims, offenders, and investigators. McDevitt and Levin found four main kinds of hate crimes, ranging from thrill-seekers, the most common, to "mission-offenders," the rare but often lethal hardcore hatemongers.

The point they were trying to make is that knowing how the minds of those who participated in hate crimes work would help law enforcement better understand the motivations and also help in catching the perpetrators quickly.

Even now, whenever there's another new hate crime case discussed on social media, many people, some even part of law enforcement, tell people not to make it all about race.

Have we made this about race, or have the people relentlessly attacked the other race for years?

There are many different types of people committing hate crimes. Some are motivated because they long for excitement and drama, which they get from bothering others most terribly. In McDevitt's study, 70 percent of these "thrill offenses" were assaults, including vicious beatings that put victims in the hospital.

Then there are the attackers who think they are being "defensive" and are harming others for goodwill to protect their religion or country. While thrill-seekers choose their victims randomly, defensive criminals target specific ones, those they know, so they can justify their actions by crying "defense."

There are also the retaliators, who commit hate crimes as revenge and as a response to personal slights. They have the mentality of eye-for-an-eye but often attack people who have nothing to do with the injustice they believe has been done against them. They only care about revenge, and it doesn't matter who they get it from as long as that person belongs to the community they want to target.

Last but not least are mission offenders. These are the rarest and deadliest hate crimes. These people have chosen to represent a single view for a racial or religious cause and will do anything to eliminate all others. They write manifestos that call on more people to join them and openly participate in hate speech.

While there has been much discussion about these types of perpetrators, how to deal with them is still unclear. However, knowing about it should be an essential part of training for law enforcement so these pointers can be used to deal with the threat of these hate crimes.

"If someone says, "I love God," and hates his brother, he is a liar; for he who does not love his brother whom he has seen, how can he love God whom he has not seen?" (1 John 4:20)

Georgia has a troubling history of racial violence, including lynchings, particularly during the late 19th and early 20th centuries. Many of these cases remain unsolved or unresolved. Here are some of the unsolved lynchings in Georgia:

Mary Turner** (1918) Mary Turner, a pregnant African American woman, was lynched in Lowndes County, Georgia, in 1918 after speaking out against the lynching of her husband. Her murder and the subsequent killings of at least six other African Americans remain unresolved, with no perpetrators brought to justice.

John "Cockey" Glover** (1921) John Glover, a black man accused of an alleged assault on a white woman, was lynched in Brooks County, Georgia, in 1921. His case, like many others during that time, was never thoroughly investigated, and those responsible for his lynching were not prosecuted.

Bud and Jesse Holmes** (1948): Bud and Jesse Holmes, two African American brothers, were found hanging from a tree in Monroe, Georgia, in 1948. Despite suspicions of foul play and calls for further investigation, their deaths were never officially classified as homicides, and the case remains unresolved.

Reverend Isaiah Nixon**(1948): Reverend Isaiah Nixon, an African American voter rights activist, was shot and killed in Montgomery County, Georgia, in 1948 after voting in a primary election. Despite evidence of racial motivation in his murder, no one was held accountable for his death.

Tom Wooster (1919)** Tom Wooster, a black man accused of attacking a white woman, was lynched in LaGrange, Georgia, in 1919. His lynching, like many others in the state during that time, went unpunished, and his case remains unresolved.

These are just a few examples of unsolved lynchings in Georgia that reflect a dark period in the state's history. Efforts are underway by historians, activists, and communities to acknowledge and confront this legacy of racial violence and to seek justice for the victims of these horrific acts. The quest for truth, reconciliation, and remembrance continues to be an essential part of addressing these unresolved cases from Georgia's past.

That's why I authored House Bill 1555.

Georgia House Bill 1555, also known as the "Cold Case Lynching Commission" bill, is a legislative initiative aimed at addressing unsolved and unpunished racial lynchings in the state. I Introduced the bill to establish a commission to investigate and seek justice for victims of historical racist violence.

Key points about Georgia's House Bill 1555, the "Cold Case Lynching Commission" bill: Purpose: The primary goal of HB 1555 is to create a commission dedicated to examining unresolved racial lynching cases in Georgia during the late 19th and early 20th centuries. The commission would investigate these cold cases, document findings, and work towards achieving accountability for past injustices.

Historical Context. Racial lynchings were a pervasive form of violence used to terrorize African Americans and enforce racial hierarchy in the United States, including in Georgia. Many of these cases were not adequately investigated or prosecuted, leaving families and communities without closure or justice.

Investigation and Documentation. The Cold Case Lynching Commission proposed under HB 1555 would be tasked with identifying and reviewing undocumented or inadequately documented cases of racial lynchings in Georgia.

The commission would collaborate with stakeholders, historians, researchers, and community members to gather information and evidence related to these unsolved crimes.

Truth and Reconciliation. By shedding light on these historical injustices and acknowledging the trauma inflicted on victims and their descendants, the commission aims to promote truth, reconciliation, and healing.

Through its work, the commission seeks to confront Georgia's legacy of racial violence and work toward a more just and equitable future.

Community Engagement. HB 1555 emphasizes the importance of community involvement in the commission's efforts. By engaging with affected communities, descendants of victims, and advocates for social justice, the commission aims to ensure that its work is rooted in the experiences and needs of those most impacted by historical racial lynchings.

Legislative Process. The bill was introduced in the Georgia House of Representatives and received bipartisan support. If passed and signed into law, the Cold Case Lynching Commission established by HB 1555 would represent a significant step towards addressing the unresolved legacy of racial violence in Georgia and seeking accountability for past atrocities.

In summary, Georgia House Bill 1555, the "Cold Case Lynching Commission" bill, reflects ongoing efforts to confront and reckon with the historical injustices of racial lynchings in the state. By establishing a dedicated commission to investigate these cold cases, the bill aims to advance truth, reconciliation, and justice while honoring the memory of the victims of racial violence.

The bill never received a hearing or made it to the floor of the Georgia General Assembly. "NOT NECESSARY RECEIVED BUT NECESSARY!"

Chapter 8

STRATEGY IN LEADING

The Bible says I spoke as a child when I was young, but as I got older, I forgot about my childish behavior. When I was young, the community labeled me an activist. That word was strong, a stereotype. As time passed, my belief in what I was doing increased, and I realized I was doing the right thing.

As a young man, I would organize marches and protests against things we felt were unjust. I remember that we would stand outside of an establishment like City Hall or the courthouse, and we would say, "They are doing the wrong thing. They're not serving the people"—they're not doing this, and they're not doing that.

As I matured, I learned that revolution is when you speak from the outside, but evolution is when you get on the inside. Evolution helps you to embark on a journey of self-discovery—something that helps you explore the strengths and weaknesses you didn't know you had.

So I learned how to grow and evolve. There are three types of levels at which you grow as a leader. One is evolving as a leader. When you're evolving, you're learning from your mistakes and maturing. The next level is becoming a leader who gives as much as required to have the mantle, a leadership title, or a position.

The third is being able to learn and grow in your leadership. Ask yourself how you can become a better leader. Find your short-comings, because only you can be your most honest critic. This is a gift you can give yourself.

When I was young, I didn't know how to do all that. All the things we were trying to do were because we wanted to make a dif-ference, but we were attempting revolutionary protests and not on the inside, unable to do anything but shout out loud or use the power of the pen.

Even my radio show, which was number-one in the city on AMR-FM, called *Tell It Like It Is*, was not revolutionary even though I used to be quite radical. I called out the people who were either part of the establishment or not fulfilling the will of the people.

I would call them out if I believed them to be wrong. But as I have said before, I wasn't appropriately equipped to bring about the phenomenon of evolution because I hadn't grown up. We must stop pointing fingers and get the information from both sides.

"When I was a child, I spoke like a child, I thought like a child: but when I became a man, I put away my childish ways." (1 Corinthians 13:11)

One thing we've got to understand as leaders is that when we move from being an activist to being a demonstrator or someone in power, we should try not to be critical. The real challenge lies in taking the lead and bringing about a significant change when you've been given that power after being elected. Are you ready to evolve internally? Are you ready to push the boundaries to serve people? Are you ready to listen to your constituents? Do you have a vision?

An incident that helped me realize this happened when I came to the Georgia House of Representatives alongside people who were attorneys, those who were highly qualified and skilled politicians. Standing in the Georgia General Assembly chambers, I began looking out and saying, *God, why me? How did you pick me? I wonder if I'm qualified.* Although I had already learned the strategies and elements of protesting, I knew I didn't have the skills that they had.

I remember something I learned from the executive director of the Southern Christian Leadership Conference, Rev. Randall T. Osborne, a cousin of Mrs. Coretta Scott King. Rev. Osborne would teach you the philosophy to get the information. He taught me to ensure I have all the pieces of information to develop a strategy, and only then should I develop one. After that, I had to develop a plan—a direct-action plan—and to establish a record of coming back to it to see if the plan of action worked. This way, I would not repeat my mistakes.

I learned to apply those principles and to learn how to take a start in bringing about evolution of solution projects to show my self-improvement. I started learning about budgets, the billing process, and building better relationships to get the bill through a committee. I needed to do this to move the team forward.

I want you all to understand that there's another way to do things. Many people think there is division in their government and infighting among local municipalities. What they need to understand is that we're legislators, not demonstrators. Our focus is to do what we're elected to do now, and we're on a mission to go ahead and make those viable decisions, to strategize and make sure that we move the agenda forward for the people. We are here to advocate policies, not to blabber about who should do what. We are in Georgia; we are not Washington, DC.

That is what we did in the case of the citizen's arrest law. We heard the people, and we saw their tears. We could feel their heartbreak. So we strategized, came up with a plan, and demonstrated it. Luckily, we remained successful. This law was the continuation of the death of Ahmaud Arbery and the outcry that followed.

To get mammoth legislation passed as a Democrat, I had to build relationships and work across party lines. I had to build consensus relationships. You have to agree to disagree. You see, in Georgia, we can agree to disagree.

Effective leadership involves implementing various strategies to inspire and guide individuals or groups toward a common goal. Here are some key strategies for leading

Clear Vision and Direction. A leader should establish a clear vision and communicate it effectively to inspire and motivate team members. Providing a sense of purpose and direction helps align everyone towards the same goals.

Effective Communication. Communication is essential in leadership. Leaders should be able to articulate their vision, provide feedback, listen actively, and keep team members informed to foster collaboration and understanding.

Lead by Example. Leading by example means demonstrating the behavior and work ethic you expect from others. When leaders model integrity, professionalism, and dedication, it sets a standard for others to follow.

Empower and Delegate. Influential leaders empower their team members by trusting them with responsibilities and delegating tasks appropriately. Delegating tasks not only helps in achieving goals efficiently but also develops the skills and confidence of team members.

Build Relationships. Strong relationships are key to successful leadership. Building trust, showing empathy, and understanding the needs of individuals within the team can foster a positive and supportive work environment.

Embrace Diversity and Inclusion. Leaders should value and leverage the diverse perspectives, experiences, and skills of their team members. Creating an inclusive environment where everyone feels respected and valued can enhance creativity, innovation, and team performance. Adaptability and resilience leaders should be adaptable and flexible in the face of changing circumstances or challenges. Being able to pivot, make decisions quickly, and bounce back from setbacks are essential qualities in effective leadership.

Continuous Learning and Development Good leaders are committed to personal and professional growth. They seek feedback, stay abreast of industry trends, and invest in their development to enhance their leadership skills and adapt to evolving environments.

Celebrating Success and Learning from Failure Recognizing and celebrating accomplishments, both big and small, helps motivate team members and cultivate a positive culture. Similarly, learning from failures and using them as opportunities for growth and improvement is crucial for ongoing success.

Inspire and motivate leaders should inspire and motivate their team members by recognizing achievements, providing growth opportunities, and fostering a positive and engaging work environment that encourages creativity and collaboration.

By implementing these strategies and adapting them to specific contexts and challenges, leaders can effectively guide their teams toward success and create a positive impact within their organizations. You never know who you will meet on the way up; that may seem to be a nobody, but as you continue your work, they become somebody.

I am known for crossing the line, but I don't call crossing the line to build a relationship. I am known for working with Democrats and Republicans. My mother always told me that this one race is the human race. We must not build on color, race, gender, or political party; We must focus on building on the strength to be open to learning from others and grow in our relationships with one another.

One powerful example of strategies in leadership was the leadership of the civil rights movement under the leadership of Dr. King. Dr. Martin Luther King Jr., a prominent leader in the Civil Rights Movement, employed various strategies to build relationships and cultivate support within the movement.

Here are some ways Dr. King built relationships within the Civil Rights Movement. Nonviolent Philosophy. Dr. King's commitment to nonviolent resistance was a central tenet of his leadership. By advocating for nonviolent protests and civil disobedience, he sought to build relationships based on mutual respect, understanding, and dignity, even in the face of opposition and violence.

Coalition Building. Dr. King recognized the importance of building alliances across different racial, religious, and socioeconomic groups. He collaborated with various organizations, activists, and community leaders to create a broad and diverse coalition supporting civil rights.

Effective Communication. Dr. King was a powerful orator and communicator. Through his speeches, sermons, and writings, he articulated the goals and values of the Civil Rights Movement, inspiring and mobilizing individuals to join the cause and work together toward social change. Personal Relationships. Dr. King invested time and effort in establishing personal relationships with supporters, activists, and community members. By listening to their concerns, sharing their struggles, and empathizing with their experiences, he was able to build trust and solidarity within the movement.

Leading by Example. Dr. King led by example, demonstrating courage, integrity, and resilience in the face of adversity. His personal commitment to the principles of justice, equality, and nonviolence inspired others to follow his lead and stay dedicated to the cause of civil rights: empowerment and Inclusion. Dr. King empowered individuals within the movement by encouraging them to take on leadership roles, express their voices, and contribute their ideas. He believed in the importance of inclusivity and valued the diverse perspectives and contributions of all participants in the struggle for civil rights.

Strategic Planning. Dr. King and other leaders in the Civil Rights Movement conducted strategic planning and coordinated efforts to maximize impact and effectiveness. By organizing marches, boycotts, and other forms of protest, they were able to amplify their message and pressure institutions to bring about change.

Respect for Differences. Dr. King emphasized the importance of respecting and embracing diversity within the movement. He valued the unique strengths and perspectives of individuals from different backgrounds and sought to create a united front against racial injustice and discrimination.

Through his approach and strategies, Dr. Martin Luther King Jr. fostered relationships, built solidarity, and inspired a collective movement for civil rights that continues to resonate and inspire generations of activists and advocates for social justice. " We are better together!"

Chapter 9

WHAT DOES THE FUTURE HOLD FOR AFRICAN AMERICANS?

We all at some time saw cruelty growing up and had to deal with difficult circumstances in our life. A big question for America now is, What does the future hold? Growing up as persons of color in America, we have had mountains to climb daily. Every day that an African American person walks down the street, he or she is dreading the worst from racists, bigots, the bias of "well-intentioned" folks, and especially the phobias of law enforcement. The same system that has promised to protect us is what hurts us the most.

In the first year of Covid-19, when much of the world hid itself indoors, the brutal and unforgivable murder of George Floyd happened. For the first time, I saw so many people united against the prejudice and discriminatory practices of people being mistreated.

Thousands came on the streets to shout their voice against oppression. This wasn't the first time the Black Lives Matter community took action, but it was the first time I witnessed with my own eyes the dramatic escalation in the scale of how many people were on the streets voicing their anger. Soon enough, England along with other countries also found themselves facing protests from marginalized communities.

I understand the people's plight, and they have every right to be angry. Our ancestors were brought to America in chains, and their descendants now live under the chains of systemic racism. We face bias everywhere we go. Those who struggle to make it big in America still have to make ten times the effort than their white counterparts. However, sitting around and throwing in the towel just isn't ideal.

We've seen many people from our community work hard and make it big in this country. Former President Obama is one crucial example. Even during his presidency, he continued to face racial bias from his political opponents, one of whom went on to become president in 2016. Yet the man never relented but maintained his composure and strength of character. Oprah Winfrey remains one of the most highly respected talk show hosts. Michael Jordan became a living legend in his basketball career. Every single one of them has gone on to contribute to their community. These are the people who prove to us that achieving goals is not impossible, but the road ahead is not going to be easy.

The late mayor of Atlanta Maynard Jackson was a prime example that all things are possible. There is a lot of growing concern over the relevancy of Black History Month. Is it still a vehicle of change, or has it now become another generic school assignment for children? Has it managed to achieve the goals it had hoped to accomplish, or is its impact dwindling? The young generation of today are growing up in an environment of so much immersion that for them, perhaps the month may not carry as much gravity as it once did. Segregation was removed due to the hard efforts of Black and white leaders in the civil rights movement. This paved the way for integration, but there are still some issues that remain present even now.

Profound changes in race relation have occurred since the time Carter G. Woodson established his vision for Black history as a means of transformation, and I believe it is still relevant today. The Civil War did remove the chains of slavery, but we are not entirely free; we wear chains today.

Considering how much diversity there already is within the African American community today, we need the binding force of our past to help guide us in knowing where we were and how far we still have to go.

It's no secret that the white population of America has been declining in recent years, and people of color are on the rise in number. This isn't a call to alarm; this is just the reality. Our rise in numbers increases our responsibility to help establish a stronger, safer, and more productive future for our children and their families.

We can assemble all the data and make assumptions from it, but the beauty of humankind lies in how it surpasses expectations and surprises itself. There was once a time where people felt flying was limited to birds. Now we are all on planes, moving from one place to another. This even applies to us, the African American community. Many of us for quite some time thought that only a fool from our community would even consider running for President. Barack Obama defied all expectations and became our head of state, not just for one term, but two. We have athletes that have broken records, we have philanthropists that have provided protection and given a future to those in need. It's unrealistic to be a pessimist.

We must hold the Constitution of the United States accountable when we read "We the People." We must be included if we hold these truths to be self-evident, that all men are created equal, that they are endowed by their Creator with certain unalienable rights, that among these are life, liberty, and the pursuit of happiness. There is nothing impossible with God. We cannot allow the skin we are in to become our limit. My mother and father always taught me that there is one race, the human race.

"There is neither Jew nor Greek, there is neither slave nor free, there is neither male nor female; for you are all one in Christ Jesus." (Galatians 3:28)

Predicting the future for any group of people, including African Americans, involves a complex interplay of social, economic, political, and cultural factors. While it's impossible to provide a definitive answer, we can discuss some potential trends and challenges that may impact the future of African Americans.

Social Progress. The future for African Americans may see continued progress in areas such as civil rights, social justice, and representation. Efforts to address systemic racism, promote diversity and inclusion, and advance equality could positively change societal attitudes and structures.

Economic Opportunities. Economic empowerment is crucial for the future of African Americans. Increased access to education, job opportunities, entrepreneurship, and wealth-building initiatives could help narrow the wealth gap and create more economic stability and prosperity within the community.

Health and Wellness. Improving healthcare access, addressing disparities in health outcomes, and promoting overall well-being are essential for the future health of African Americans. Efforts to reduce healthcare inequities and improve mental health support could lead to better outcomes for individuals and communities.

Educational Attainment. Education plays a crucial role in shaping opportunities and outcomes for African Americans. Continued efforts to improve educational quality, address disparities in access and achievement, and support lifelong learning could enhance prospects for future generations.

Political Representation. Increasing representation and participation in political leadership positions could amplify the voices of African Americans and influence policy decisions that benefit the community. Encouraging civic engagement, voting rights protection, and advocacy for issues affecting African Americans could shape the political landscape in the future.

Cultural Influence. African-American culture has significantly contributed to various aspects of society, including art, music, literature, and media. The future may see a continuation of this cultural influence, promoting diversity, creativity, and dialogue across different communities and perspectives.

Technological Advancements. Embracing technology and digital innovation can create opportunities for African Americans to engage in new sectors, industries, and modes of communication.

Closing the digital divide, promoting digital literacy, and leveraging technology for empowerment and advancement could be critical for the future.

Community Empowerment. Building strong communities, supporting grassroots initiatives, and fostering collaboration and solidarity within the African-American community can enhance resilience, unity, and collective well-being for the future.

While there are challenges and uncertainties ahead, proactive efforts to address issues of inequality, promote inclusion, and create opportunities for advancement can shape a more promising future for African Americans. It will require collective action, policy changes, and ongoing commitment to justice and equity to realize a future where all individuals, regardless of race, have the opportunity to thrive and succeed. If we want to get there, look at these various states outlines of the demographics of African Americans:

As of 2023, the demographic breakdown of African Americans in the states of Georgia, South Carolina, Florida, and North Carolina are as follows: Georgia: African American population: Approximately 32.6% of the total population. Georgia has one of the highest percentages of African Americans in the United States. South Carolina: African American population: Approximately 27.1% of the total population. South Carolina has a significant African American population, particularly in certain regions of Florida. African American population: Approximately 16.9% of the total population. Florida's African American population is spread throughout the state, with concentrations in urban areas such as Miami, Tampa, and Jacksonville. North Carolina: African American population: Approximately 21.5% of the total population. North Carolina has a sizable African American population, especially in cities like Charlotte, Raleigh, and Greensboro.

It is important to note that these states have rich histories and diverse communities, with African Americans playing a significant role in shaping their cultural, social, and political landscapes. It is also important to note that if these percentages represent each state, the minority participation rate should be equal.

The percentage of the elected positions should be equal. It will take the entire village to collectively come together to change these obstacles and move us from what is without to be.

Chapter 10

MOVING FROM WHAT IS TO WHAT OUGHT TO BE

I've been around for enough time to see where my community was when I was born and to where it is today. Looking back, although we have managed to make many strides to improve our well-being and to be respected as citizens in this country, I can't help but notice how oddly slow our progress has been. Considering recent events such as the BLM movement, I sometimes wonder whether we've even managed to address the core roots of discrimination and prejudice set against us.

In 1940, 60 percent of employed Black women were working as domestic servants; as of today, that number has dropped down to 2.2 percent, while 60 percent are employed in white-collar jobs. That is certainly an improvement. In 1958, 44 percent of whites would openly say that they would move out of the neighborhood if a Black family moved in. Today, that is down to 1 percent. No denying that there has been improvement there. In 1964, the Civil Rights Act was passed, during a time when only 18 percent of whites claimed to have a friend who was Black; as of now, 86 percent claim that they have a Black friend, while 87 percent of Black people say they have white friends. I don't doubt these figures show that there has been some improvement, but the facts basically serve as a media report while the Black underclass continues to be the representative of their community in America.

The thinking remains that Blacks live in ghettos, mostly in high-rise public housing projects. Crime and welfare checks remain their source of income rather than well-paying jobs in different fields. These stereotypes aren't fixed in the white community only; in fact, they cross racial lines. Asians and Hispanics, although subject to their own share of bias, also view the Black community as such.

There is no denying that about fifty years ago, most of the Black community was trapped in poverty, but they didn't reside in inner cities at the time. In fact, most African Americans were located in the South and on the land as laborers and sharecroppers. It wasn't common to find Blacks who even owned land. Those who weren't enduring hard labor were mostly involved in non-manual, white-collar work of any kind, and unsurprisingly they were ill-paid, insecure, manual jobs—job that few whites would take. As we already know, six out of ten Black women were household servants, who due to economic desperation often worked twelve-hour days for ridiculously low earnings. Segregation in the South and discrimination in the North resulted in the formation of a sheltered market for a few Black businesses. This included enterprises such as beauty parlors, funeral homes, and others. This maintained something of an invisible line where Blacks were kept separate. Yet the number was still small.

When the 1940s came around, the country began to experience a certain series of changes, some of which could be attributed to World War II and changing realities. The economy and demographics were beginning to take a different route, which came alongside a marked shift in racial attitudes. This formed the stepping-stones to Blacks starting to take more measures in fighting for equality.

The New Deal legislation had set minimum wages and hours and removed the incentive of southern employers to hire low-wage Black workers, which certainly slowed industrial development in the region. The further weakening of the South was due to the shift toward mechanized agriculture and a dying demand for American cotton due to intense international competition, along with displacing Blacks from the land.

These changes had their benefits and their cons as well. With World War II already in high gear and a shortage of workers growing in northern manufacturing plants, southern-based Blacks started making their way toward the North. This event would become known as the Great Migration, which continued till the mid-1960s. By that time, Black workers had managed to find high wages, receiving double the amount they would have back in 1953.

During the 1950s, wages continued growing, and unemployment lessened.

By the time 1960 came around, one out of seven Black men were still working as laborers, and almost a quarter were in white-collar or skilled manual-labor jobs. Twenty-four percent had semi-skill-based jobs that automatically brought them into the middle class.

Black women who worked as servants were now reduced to half in number.

In 1970, the increase of wages was becoming even more visible. For about thirty years leading to that time, Black men had cut the income gap by about a third and were now earning up to 60 percent of what white men were. Life expectancy had shot up along with home ownership. College enrollment rose to about 10 percent, whereas prior to war it was 1 percent. As the years continued, the pace increased, but at a steadier rate. An example of this is that today, more than 30 percent of Black men and nearly 60 percent of Black women are employed in white-collar occupations. This is a stark contrast from back in the 1970s when only 2.2 percent of American physicians were Black, compared to 4.5 percent today.

Having seen the statistics, there is something that strikes one as odd. Many of us wonder what the future holds for the Black community, but the only way to be sure is to look back, and one thing stands out. In the post–world war era, our people began to experience certain improvements, but somewhere in between, a certain stagnation began to occur. The stagnation appeared to show around the same time affirmative action was initiated.

Between 1970 and 1990, the number of physicians tripled, the number of engineers quadrupled, and the number of attorneys increased about sixfold. This reflects that during those years, America's professional schools changed their admissions criteria for Black applicants, accepting and providing financial aid to African American students whose academic records were much lower than those of many white and Asian American applicants whom these schools were turning away.

The mentioned professionals only amount to a small fraction of the total Black middle class. If anything, the stagnation and growth should not have occurred, so somewhere along the lines, something went wrong. The best economic gains were achieved from the 1960s to 1975, but the surrounding reality was quite mixed. The Blacks continued to face discrimination on job opportunities, and although they were earning comparatively higher, little was done in regards to health, education, and security for the community.

The hovering question comes down to why that's the case. What stalled the movement of progress? Since the affirmative action policies were initiated, the poverty rate remained pretty much the same. Black people did garner some success in other measures, yet 30 percent of families still live under the poverty line.

What emerges as an obstacle is persistent inequality, which is a byproduct of discrimination, and the only way to combat those are race-conscious remedies. In the 1960s, racism was generally expected to come from whites, but today the situation has become complex.

The fact that an equal amount of white and Black students attend college and graduate around the same time reveals that Blacks are not equally educated like whites. The National Assessment of Educational Progress (NAEP) is the nation's report card on what American students attending elementary and secondary schools know. Those tests show that African American students, on average, are alarmingly far behind whites in math, science, reading, and writing. For instance, Black students at the end of their high school career are almost four years behind white students in reading; the gap is comparable in other subjects.

A study of 26- to 33-year-old men who held full-time jobs in 1991 thus found that when education was measured by years of school completed, Blacks earned 19 percent less than comparably educated whites. But when word knowledge, paragraph comprehension, arithmetical reasoning, and mathematical knowledge became the yardstick, the results were reversed. Black men earned 9 percent more than white men with the same education—that is, the same performance on basic tests.

It's difficult to pin down as to why there is such a glaring racial gap in levels of educational attainment. The concern is the gap itself. What is more worrisome is that we have to face that in recent years, it's only increasing.

In 1971, the average African American seventeen-year-old couldn't read better than any other white kid who was six years younger. The racial gap in math during 1973 was 4.3 years, whereas in science it was 4.7 in 1970. By the late 1980s, the stats rose further. Black students in their final year of high school were only 2.5 years behind whites in both reading and math and 2.1 years behind on tests of writing skills.

If the pace of progress had continued to improve, then today Black students would be performing about as well as their white classmates. Instead, the improvement slowly declined, and backsliding came in between. Even now, not many experts are sure as to what has led to this situation. Only speculation runs amok, with little factual explanation. The early gains that were experienced years back had a lot to do with the growth of the Black middle class, but the Black middle class did not suddenly begin to shrink in the late 1980s. The poverty rate was not dropping significantly when educational progress was occurring, nor was it on the increase when the racial gap began once again to increase.

There has been a rise in out-of-wedlock births, and the steep and steady decline in the proportion of Black children growing up with two parents doesn't explain the fluctuating educational performance of African-American children. Children raised in single-parent homes perform less well in schools than others, regardless of whether other variables, such as income, are maintained. All the more reason why there are more questions than there are answers.

Despite a lot of what is mentioned, I still find myself believing that there is hope for the Black community in the future. Now, this may come as a surprise, but there are certain things being overlooked. It is completely understandable that since the events of George Floyd's killing, a lot of fear and paranoia has spread across the country. Police continue to be frightening sources of worry, but at the same time, the BLM movement has spread in a manner unlike ever before. When people took to the streets, a nationwide and even international movement followed that spread to countries who were once colonizers. England found itself seeing marches from the subcontinent community, which included Pakistanis, Indians, Bengalis, and others, who were lashing out against the discrimination they faced during colonial rule and the "desi beatings" during the 1980s. Other countries followed suit, and this reflects that marginalized communities aren't going to tolerate any more discrimination. They are taking their anger to the streets and venting their anger out.

That is the display of a domino effect in which Black people have stood up for themselves. There is enough awareness now, especially among the younger generation, about how systemic racism works, and they are quick to call it out. These are steps slowly taking hold to overcome the hindrances that prevent Black people from advancing. When it comes to education, that is where a collective effort is needed. Without banding together and keeping ourselves divided on petty issues, we can't go far. Too much has already happened and is continuing to happen.

If we are to change things for the better, then we need to be willing to face the obstacles that come our way. There are plenty in this country who would rather keep the status quo. Those are the ones the people need to be willing to face. The difficulties that come with that are going to be slow and arduous, but it's important to maintain the sight of the goal.

Giving up is too easy, and being a pessimist is unrealistic. For everything bad that happens, there are always going to be those who will be doing good and striving for better things. After the death of George Floyd, countless people stood up, and their demands for betterment will push deep into economic, social, and political matters.

As long as the Black community remains consistent and starts now, then perhaps two or three generations down, we might witness an America in which our grandchildren have better opportunities to excel because ancestors put in the work to pave the way. I don't expect it to be some romanticized utopia—there will still be discrimination and prejudice—but at least we can bring the system to a point where that can be controlled and those endorsing trouble are punished.

America is in a bad place right now, and bad times create strong people. The steps of change have already ignited the spark, causing an explosion. Now we stand at the precipice of healing those that are hurt and starting anew. It's time to move from what is to what ought to be.

"For as we have many members in one body, but all the members do not have the same function, so we, being many, are one body in Christ, and individually members of one another.⁶ Having then gifts differing according to the grace that is given to us, let us use them: if prophecy, let us prophesy in proportion to our faith;"
(Romans 12:4-6)

"Be of the same mind toward one another. Do not set your mind on high things, but associate with the humble. Do not be wise in your own opinion. Repay no one evil for evil. Have regard for good things in the sight of all men." (Romans 12:16-17)

"I in them, and You in Me; that they may be made perfect in one, and that the world may know that You have sent Me, and have loved them as You have loved Me. (John 17:23)

"So let it be written, so let it be done."
–Cecil B. Demille

WRITE THE VISION NOTES

_____

_____

_____

_____

_____

_____

_____

_____

_____

_____

_____

_____

_____

_____

_____

_____

_____

ABOUT THE AUTHOR

Dr. Carl W. Scott Gilliard is a national leader who currently serves as a State Representative in the Georgia General Assembly as Chairman of the Georgia Legislative Black Caucus, the largest black caucus in the world. He is an author, filmmaker, and noted national speaker. Dr. Gilliard is also the CEO and founder of Feed The Hungry, Inc. Since 2009, his organization has fed 1.5 million meals in 14 cities in both Georgia and South Carolina. Dr. Gilliard is known as "James Brown" of the Georgia General Assembly, one of the hardest-working leaders in the nation. He is responsible for authoring mammoth legislation to repeal Georgia's citizen arrest law, The Blind Bill, The Weeping Time Heritage Corridor, and the Gullah Geechee Heritage Society. He has been featured on the Daily Show with Trevor Noah, Roland Martin, GPB's Lawmakers, and the Washington Post Descendants.